A GENEALOGICAL HISTORY

OF THE

FICKLIN FAMILY

From the First of the Name in America
to the Present Time, with some Account
of the Family in England   ::   ::   ::

COMPILED BY

WALTER HOMAN FICKLIN

TO MY LITTLE SON, JOSEPH KENMUIR FICKLIN,
AND HIS COUSINS, WHO MAY SOME DAY BE IN
QUEST OF SUCH INFORMATION AS THAT
HEREIN CONTAINED, THIS BOOK IS
AFFECTIONATELY INSCRIBED.

CONTENTS.

LIST OF ENGRAVINGS.

———

PREFACE.

Eleven years ago, the writer, actuated by curiosity, began to inquire concerning his Ficklin antecedents. In a short time the research became to him a most absorbing and fascinating pastime, though for the first few years his labors resulted in a scant collection of disconnected data concerning late generations together with a few facts and more fiction concerning the older ones. About that time the task of getting together anything like a complete history of the family, showing the connection between the first immigrant and the present generation of all branches, appeared to be a hopeless task and was so regarded by others. The condition of public records, described elsewhere, together with the fact that but one very brief account of the family existed and that applying almost exclusively to one branch, appeared to preclude success.

It occurred to the writer that some one should, without delay, collect up such information as was still available, for with the lapse of time and the passing of the older generations, unrecorded family history is lost or incorrectly handed down. The information this volume contains, meagre as it is, perhaps might never be again assembled, even though some kinsman in a future generation may be disposed to assume the task.

The writer has been asked to explain in this publication his methods of research. As this would require considerable space, any reader who may be contemplating such work is urged to consult Henry R. Stiles' "Hand-book of Practical Suggestions for the Use of Students in Genealogy," published by Joel Munsell's Sons, Albany, N. Y. The writer's experience differs little from that of thousands of others engaged in similar work. Had he known of Mr. Stiles' book in time, it would have saved him much trouble and expense, for it is all that its title suggests.

In order to get facts, each clew was followed persistently, for years if necessary, till it yielded its fruit or vanished into nothingness. These clews led along very devious paths. By means of considerable advertising and a voluminous correspondence, the material in this book was gathered, bit by bit, from the following sources: members of the family still living, old letters or manuscripts, family Bibles, epitaphs, church registers, newspaper clippings, town, county and state histories, records of allied families, genealogical publications, census returns, wills, deeds, marriage records, records of court proceedings, and archives in the colonial land offices, the Pension office, and U. S. War Department.

Most unfortunately the older county records in Virginia, consisting of wills, deeds, etc., are in a deplorable state. Those which escaped the depredations of the British soldiers during the War of the Revolution were depleted by Federal soldiers during the Civil War. Early church registers, showing marriages, births, baptisms, and deaths, shared the same fate. The returns for Virginia and Kentucky, and several other states, at the Federal census of 1790, and also that of 1800, were destroyed when the British troops burned the National Capitol, 24 August, 1814.

The first two or three generations of Ficklins in Virginia resided in King George, Spottsylvania, Stafford, and Culpeper counties. No returns for any of these, excepting Stafford, at the Virginia Census, 1782-85, can be found. The above counties, being between Washington and Richmond, were occupied and traversed by immense armies from 1861 to 1865, and were the scene of several of the major battles of the Civil War, such as Fredericksburg, Chancellorsville, Spottsylvania, and the Wilderness, besides innumerable minor engagements and raids.

Nearly all of the older family Bibles of the Ficklins, likewise old portraits and papers, have been destroyed or lost by burning of residences during the Civil War.

Very fortunately two old documents escaped destruction, one is an old deed on record in King George, dated 1756, in which are mentioned the names of the first Ficklin in Virginia and his entire family. The other is a very brief manuscript account of the family (alluded to above) prepared about 1860 by a member of an allied family, William Slaughter of Fredericksburg, Virginia. This was published, with a few additions, by Slaughter W. Ficklin at Charlottesville, Virginia, in 1870, and entitled, "Genealogy of the Ficklin Family Since 1720." The original manuscript of William Slaughter is in the possession of his grandson, Harry C. Ficklen, of Danville, Virginia, who has furnished the writer with an exact copy. This has been constantly consulted and is published in part in this volume. The deed corrects an important error in the manuscript, but otherwise they supplement each other.

It is to be regretted that ill health and untimely death prevented Slaughter W. Ficklin from supplementing his pamphlet of 1870 by a more complete account of the family which he was contemplating. Thus was lost that great store of information possessed by him and that which was available from members of older generations then living, but who have since passed away.

Many years may elapse before the English ancestor of the American branch of the family is identified. It is therefore deemed best to delay no longer the publication of all available history of that branch.

WALTER H. FICKLIN.

Littleton, Colorado, 10 January, 1912.

CHAPTER I.

A SURVEY OF THE FICKLIN FAMILY IN AMERICA.

It has been the writer's privilege to have a much wider acquaintance with his own living relatives, near and distant, than falls to the lot of most people. Much correspondence and research has given him a glimpse into the lives of many of those in the generations which have gone before.

The family has been one of pioneers. Stout-hearted men and women were those who peopled the American colonies, for of the thousands who risked their lives in passage hither, but few ever beheld their native land again, and in those days the transit of messages was so uncertain and slow that many never heard from or of their relatives again. Such was probably the case with the Ficklin immigrant to Virginia whom we find, at the first glimpse of him, living in what was then a new country, King George county, Virginia, where he made his home.

His sons, when grown, began to scatter to newer country westward. Several of his grandsons started for Kentucky in the vanguard of civilization when that region was "The Dark and Bloody Ground," and were associated with Boone, Harrod, the Todds, Craigs and others in that bloody struggle with the Indians at the close of the Revolution. Here we find all the sons of the second William, excepting the one who died in the army in 1777. Thomas and his family were in Bryant's Station in 1782 during the memorable siege. John and his family were a few miles away in a very thinly settled portion of Jessamine county. Joseph is thought to have gone to Kentucky with his brothers, but the first record of him is in 1797, when he was one of the first party of whites to settle in what is now Allen county. About 1798, John, son of Thomas, settled in Mason county, and Daniel, son of Benjamin, settled in Fleming county. Unfortunately little record can be found of the personal experiences of any of these excepting what is indicated by the early history of these regions. It is sufficient to say that not one of them turned back. They spent the remainder of their lives where they had settled.

There is a belief prevalent among certain members of the family that, during the Revolution, the Ficklins were without exception proud and consistent Tories. Some may have been, for the writer is informed that Lippincott's "Legends of the Revolutionary War" relates a tradition that one of the South Carolina Ficklings, who was a Tory, was captured by patriots, who proceeded at once to hang him. The rope broke three times, however, and superstition coming to the rescue, he was released.

A glance at the roster of soldiers, published below, will show that at least two of the Virginia Ficklins served in the Continental army, and that four Ficklings served in a single South Carolina regiment. Doubtless others of the family served either in the army or in the militia, though the fragments of records still in existence do not reveal it. It would have been difficult for able-bodied men to have escaped service entirely.

We find three of the Kentucky Ficklins, of a later generation, in the Battle of the Thames, where Tecumseh fell. There is little doubt that these were also present at Dudley's defeat and the Massacre at Fort Meigs, a year before.

In the settlement of the West the Ficklins are found among the "49ers" who hunted gold in California, and others, who with ox team bravely encountered every conceivable hardship and danger, crossed the Great American desert, threaded their way through the rocky defiles of the mountains, and did not stop till they reached the Pacific.

Ben Ficklin, a great grandson of William, immigrant, was a noted plainsman, who carried the first U. S. mail from Independence, Mo., across the continent to San Francisco. His skill and dauntless courage in operating his "Pony Express," and other stage lines in regions infested with redskins and outlaws, was a great factor in the settlement of the Southwest in the days before the Civil War.

Nearly all the Ficklins lived in the South during the Civil War, were in the main slave holders, and very largely cast their lot with the Confederacy, and in its armies the family was exceedingly well represented from First Manassas to the death grapple at Appomattox. As a result of the abrupt liberation of the slaves, together with depreciation of land values, confiscation and destruction of property, the conflict proved to be a great blow to the family in general and to allied families.

In the two centuries which have passed since the Ficklin family was transplanted to the soil of Virginia, it has become well Americanized, and several hundred descendents of the original immigrant have spread his name from the Atlantic to the Pacific.

The Ficklins have, of course, followed various vocations, sometimes exalted, sometimes humble, but always honorable. They have been, with few exceptions, inclined to mercantile and agricultural pursuits rather than the learned professions or politics. It is not to be concluded, however, that the family has not been well represented in the professions. Orlando Bell Ficklin, of Illinois, was a lawyer of national reputation; John Rose Ficklen, of Tulane University, was a widely known author and student of history; Joseph Ficklin, of the University of Missouri, was a mathematician and author whose biography appears among those of noted Americans in Appleton's Encyclopedia of American Biography. Only one or two have taken up army life or life in the navy as a calling, though they have at all times responded unflinchingly to their country's call, and many have perished on battlefields far from home and fireside.

The immigrant and his family were probably members of the Episcopal church in which were many of his descendants, as shown by the Reverend Philip Slaughter's "St. Mark's Parish" and "St. George's Parish," and Bishop Meade's "Old Churches." Some of his grandsons were staunch Baptists and Methodists. At the present time his descendants may be found in nearly all Protestant denominations in which two or three have been ministers of the gospel.

Slaughter W. Ficklin, in his pamphlet of 1870, remarks concerning the family: "They are moral, generally religious, of unimpeachable integrity, good citizens, fast friends and stern opponents of wrong and oppression. * * * They have never been noted for taciturnity; but, on the other hand, have always done their full share of talking whenever talking was allowable."

CHAPTER II.

GLEANINGS.

Joseph Ficklin (No. 36), who was appointed postmaster at Lexington, Ky., in 1822, is believed to have held the office longer and through more presidential administrations than any other postmaster in this country.—Ranke's History of Lexington.

Benjamin Ficklin (No. 98) carried the first United States mail across the continent to San Francisco, in 1852. Some account of his experience as manager of the famous "Pony Express" may be found in Root and Connelly's "Overland Stage to California," Topeka, 1901. Some account of his part in the Civil War may be found in Wilkerson's "Recollections of a Blockade-Runner."

In the Illinois Law Review for January, 1907, is an interesting account of the Matson Slave case (1847), in which Orlando B. Ficklin (No. 108) and Abraham Lincoln were opposing counsel. The Charleston, Ill., Courier for 18 September, 1908, gives a detailed account of the famous Lincoln-Douglas debate at that place in 1858, at which Orlando B. Ficklin, a friend of both, presided.

In volume twelve of the Filson Club Publications (Louisville, Ky.) is a detailed account of the defense of Bryant's Station against Indians, in 1782, in which Thomas Ficklin (No. 9) and family participated.

Joseph Ficklin (No. 128) and Thomas A. Ficklin (see No. 106) crossed the Plains to California in 1849, in search of gold. The former perished in the gold camps.

Wood's History of Albemarle County, Virginia, contains an account of how Benjamin Ficklin (No. 30) compelled the observance of law in Charlottesville in an early day.

Theodore H. Ficklin (No. 336) was lieutenant colonel of the 40th Virginia Infantry when that regiment surrendered with General Lee at Appomattox, 9 April, 1865.

James Burwell Ficklen (No. 167) participated in the capture of John Brown at Harper's Ferry, Virginia, 16 October, 1859.

More members of the Ficklin family have resided in Fredericksburg, Virginia, than at any other place in America.

William Threlkill Ficklen (No. 227), born 16 September, 1827, residing at Paris, Kentucky, is thought to be the senior member of the Ficklin family in America (1912).

"Ben Ficklin," a town named in honor of Benjamin Ficklin, the Plainsman, was formerly the county-seat of Greene county, Texas. The town, however, was completely destroyed by a flood a few years ago, and never rebuilt. San Angelo is at present the seat of government.

A town in Douglas county, Illinois, is named "Ficklin" in honor of Orlando B. Ficklin. A town of the same name in Wilkes county, Georgia, was named for Dr. Fielding Ficklen.

"Fickling" is a village in Taylor county, Georgia.

One of the most conspicuous of the Ficklings was Francis William Fickling, of Columbia, S. C., 1811-1887, an account of whom is contained in the National Encyclopedia of American Biography, vol. 6, p. 121.

CHAPTER III.

A PARTIAL ROSTER OF SOLDIERS.

(The following list is given with the knowledge that it consists of probably only a small percentage of the members of the Ficklin family who at some time served their country as soldiers.)

WAR OF THE REVOLUTION.

Charles Ficklin (No. 12) was a private in Captain John Spottswood's Company of the 10th Virginia Regiment, commanded by Colonel Edward Stevens. He died in the service in September, 1777.

John Ficklin (No. 10), brother of the above, was a private in Capt. Wm. Taliaferro's Company, Col. Wm. Woodford's Regiment of Virginia Troops.

Joseph Fickling, Sr., was captain of a hundred, Col. Joseph Glover's Reg't, Colleton Co., S. C., foot. This company was raised in the Edisto Island district, 1776. *Joseph Fickling, Jr.*, was second lieutenant, and *Jeremiah* and *John Fickling* were privates, in Capt. Joseph Jenkins' company of Col. Glover's regiment. Uniform, "Blue Coat with white Cuffs and Lappels with Jacketts & Breeches of white with Fann Tail Hatt."—So. Carolina Hist. and Gen. Magazine, vol. 2, 1901.

WAR OF 1812-14.

John Ficklin (No. 42) was a corporal in Capt. James C. Price's Company of the Lewis Regiment of Kentucky Volunteers.

Thomas Ficklin (No. 44) was a private in Captain Mason Singleton's Company of Col. Trotter's Regiment of Kentucky Volunteers.

John H. Ficklin (No. 35) was a private in Capt. Jacob Stucker's Company, Richard M. Johnson's Regiment of Kentucky mounted infantry.

All the above regiments were in the Battle of the Thames and other campaigns of this war.

BLACK HAWK WAR.

Orlando B. Ficklin (No. 108) was quartermaster in Captain Jordan's Company of Illinois Troops, Black Hawk War, 1832.

WAR WITH MEXICO.

John Ficklin (No. 125) was a soldier among the Kentucky troops. His brother, *Thomas (No. 129)* was with him and was killed at Matamoras.

THE CIVIL WAR.

John Ficklin (No. 125) was a colonel of a battalion of Kentucky infantry, C. S. A., bearing his name.

Theo. H. Ficklin (No. 336) was lieutenant colonel of the 40th Virginia Volunteer Infantry.

S. W. Ficklin (No. 94) was captain and assistant quartermaster, C. S. A.

Benjamin F. Ficklin (No. 98) was quartermaster of Stonewall Jackson's corps, C. S. A., and afterwards operated a blockade runner.

B. R. Ficklin (not identified) was lieutenant colonel 45th Virginia Infantry, C. S. A.

Joseph E. Ficklin (No. 176) was major 51st Virginia Infantry, C. S. A.

William L. Ficklin (See No. 70) was 2nd lieutenant 4th Virginia Cavalry, C. S. A., known as "Black Horse."

Thomas D. Ficklin (No. 333) was 1st lieutenant in the 40th Virginia Infantry, C. S. A.

Joseph B. Ficklen (probably No. 181 or 189) was surgeon, C. S. A.

William Ficklin (No. 332) served in the 9th Virginia Cavalry, C. S. A.

Eugene Ficklin (No. 335) served in the 40th Virginia Infantry, C. S. A., and was wounded at Bull Run.

James B. Ficklen (No. 167) was a member of the Richmond Howitzers, commanded by Maj. Geo. W. Randolph.

E. S. Fickling was a lieutenant 1st South Carolina Artillery, C. S. A.

William W. Fickling was a captain of South Carolina Artillery, C. S. A.

D. B. Fickling was a captain, 28th Battery Georgia Artillery, C. S. A.

W. H. Fickling was major, 59th Georgia Infantry, C. S. A.

Nicholas F. Ficklin (No. 291) was a gunner in Capt. Churchill Clark's Battery (Mo.), C. S. A. Taken prisoner at Bolivar Landing, Mississippi, 1863, confined for two years at Camp Morton, Indiana.

Robert Ficklin (No. 290) was a member of "Merrill's Horse," a command of Federal Cavalry (Missouri), and was killed at Little Rock, September 9th, 1863.

Joseph Ficklin (No. 111) was, at fifty years of age, a member of the body guard of Gen. Sterling Price, 1861-62.

James W. Ficklin (No. 275) was a Confederate soldier (Missouri, exact organization unknown), served throughout the war and surrendered in North Carolina.

Thomas A. Ficklin (See No. 106) was a Confederate soldier (Texas), exact organization not known.

John Ficklin (See No. 70) was a member of Company H, 4th Virginia Cavalry, C. S. A., known as "The Black Horse," and was killed at the Battle of Travillian Station.

William Henry Fickling, son of Jacob Fickling, of Henry county, Illinois, was among the Federal troops at Vicksburg. 11 April, 1864, he was accidentally shot by a comrade. He was seventeen years of age.

CHAPTER IV.

SOME ACCOUNT OF THE FICKLIN FAMILY IN ENGLAND.

Old records show that members of the Ficklin family have lived in Norfolk and Suffolk counties in England for upward of six centuries. Those residing in other parts of that country sprang from these places. There are a large number of families living in Norfolk county at the present time who spell the name *Fickling*. Others spell it *Ficklin*, and a few, *Ficklen*. Norfolk and Suffolk are in the east of England on the North Sea. The city of Norwich and vicinity appears to have been the original home of the family.

The following clipping from the Norfolk Chronicle and Norwich Gazette, being a response by Mr. Walter Rye (an English Historian living in Norwich), to a query inserted in that paper by the writer, will be of interest in this connection:

"Ficklin Family.—In answer to your American correspondent's query, I append a copy of my notes as to this name. It is a common one in Norfolk and Suffolk, and, *prima facie*, is a diminutive of the personal name, 'Fick' or 'Fycke,' which is not in itself uncommon, *e. g.*, Thos. Fyke, of W. Dereham, in 1309; John Fycke, freeman of Norwich, in 1462. On the other hand, it may be a variant of either 'Filkin' or 'Fitlyng'; the latter may be a misreading, 't' and 'c' being very like in early writing. * * * The first time I have found the name in its present form is about 1279, when Wm. Fickelyn was witness to a charter, probably before 7 Ed. I., to the Abbot and Convent of Leiston, of land in Knodishall, etc., in Suffolk (Pat. Roll, 19 Ed. II., p. 207). From 1380-1 (4 Richd. II.), when Thomas Ficlyng, fisherman, was admitted a freeman of Norwich, the name constantly appears here, *e. g.*, in 1616, Robert Fickelinge, cordwainer, was admitted here after an apprenticeship, and Christopher Fickelinge—probably his father. The Widow Ficklyn paid rates at Heigham, 1633-4. In 1642, Nicholas, son of Robert Fickling, tailor, was admitted, and in 1662 and 1664 the wills of two John Ficklings were proved at Norwich. Your correspondent should have the Heigham register, and these and other wills searched. No arms were ever registered to the name; but at Frenze, Blomefield (i. p. 142), says they were once granted by Tindall, whose coat was impaled by Hagsett, but he does not blazon them, and I do not know what they were supposed to be. Mr. Berney Ficklin, of Tasburgh, who assumed the name (his patronymic being Brown) has a female descent from a Ficklin of Suffolk."

The writer believes no extended account of the family in England exists. He has had wide correspondence with members of the family in that country and also with genealogists. A London bookdealer, who makes a specialty of books, manuscripts, etc., pertaining to family history can find no trace of any such record.

Benjamin Fickling, of Ennismare Arms, London, recently sent the writer a twenty-eight page pamphlet, an autobiography entitled "The History of Jacob Fickling." This is taken up mainly with the events in the life of Jacob Fickling, who was born in Norfolk county, England, 6 February, 1812, and sailed from London in 1844—destination, Quebec. He afterwards settled at East Cambridge, in Henry county, Illinois, where he reared a large family. He returned to London and died there in 1906, at age of 94. He traces his ancestry as far as his grandfather, Nathan Fickling, who resided at Fersfield, near Diss, in Norfolk county. The pamphlet mentions no collateral branches.

Philip Berney Ficklin of Tasburgh Hall, near Norwich, is a great[2] grandson of Robert Ficklin of Hadleigh in Suffolk, whose wife was Ann, daughter of Col. John Farewell of Toppesfield Hall in Essex. Robert Ficklin died in February, 1788, aged about eighty, and is buried at Hadleigh. He was a contemporary of the immigrant to Virginia.

Benjamin Fickling of London, nephew of Jacob Fickling, mentioned above, mentions in a letter some of the characteristics of the Ficklings in England:

"As a rule we are short, well-built men, round features, ruddy complexion, short thick necks, rather prominent nasal organs, a plentiful crop of dark curly hair—we never get bald and it does not turn color until an advanced age. We are quick-witted and dearly love a sparkling repartee, which is always given with a merry twinkle of the eye. We are very muscular—chest well developed. We are fond of all out-of-door sports, and seldom go to a theatre or an in-door place of amusement—scrupulously clean in our persons, and dress neatly and well—fond of home life (large families are prevalent) —generous to a friend—always respected by our fellows, a good friend and a bad enemy.

"One striking peculiarity is that we always look younger than we are. We have acute hearing and good eyesight. Sickness seldom troubles us.

"I have been many times astounded at the facial resemblance of the family. I have met many Ficklings, in no way related to me that I could learn, who were marvelously like members of my own family, and, while on a visit to the United States about nine years since, I was struck particularly with the strong resemblance my American relatives showed to their English ones.

"We are slow to anger, but when thoroughly aroused, passion breaks forth like a tornado. We are masterful and resent subjection of any kind. We are plodders and generally successful in all our undertakings. We are blessed with a retentive memory and seldom forget a name, face, or date."

The writer regrets that more information concerning the family in England is not at his disposal. The synopsis of some of the old records in Norfolk and Suffolk, which mention the Ficklins, published elsewhere in this volume, indicates that therein lies a broad field of research, which if it revealed but a fragmentary and wholly disconnected history of the family, would yet furnish a large volume of very quaint, interesting and instructive facts. It is to be hoped that some member of the family in that country may undertake the work of gathering together whatever there is of general or special interest and follow the surname through its changes till it disappears in the mists of the past.

CHAPTER V.

___

ARMORIAL BEARINGS.*

___

After careful inquiry and search, the writer is convinced that arms have been granted in centuries past to very few of the Ficklins in England. Upon request, Mr. Walter Rye of Norwich made a search of the many comprehensive works on heraldry to which he has access and with which he is familiar. Neither Burke nor Edmundson mention the name in their armories, nor is it mentioned in three Norfolk armories. A similar search was made by Mr. Joseph H. Tyrrell, of Twickenham, but with the same result, excepting that a Fickling crest is shown in Knight and Butters' "Family Crests," and described as follows: "On a chapeau, gules (red), turned up, ermine, an eagle's head, azure." Two Fickling crests, that just described and one other, an eagle's

head only, are shown on plates 96 and 100, respectively, in Fairbairn's "Crests of Great Britain and Ireland." In Mr. Rye's newspaper response, quoted above, will be noted: "No arms were ever registered to the name; but at Frenze, Blomefield (i. p. 142), says they were once granted by Tindall, whose coat was impaled by Hagsett, but he does not blazon them, and I do not know what they were supposed to be." (The publication referred to by Mr. Rye is probably Blomefield's eleven volume history of Norfolk.)

Benjamin Fickling of London writes that one of his ancestors took out armorial bearings at the College of Arms in London. His crest is doubtless one of those shown in Fairbairn.

___

*A coat of arms is and remains the exclusive property of that person who established his prescriptive right to it—being a gentleman of the old race—or received it in more recent times by royal deed of concession. Only his lineal descendants, *not* his collateral relatives, can pretend to it; and his own brother is no more entitled to it than any other confessed pretender.—E. de Vermont, in AMERICAN HERALDICA.

CHAPTER VI.

ORIGIN AND SPELLING OF SURNAME, FICKLIN.

To any one who has given study to the origin of surnames, it is readily understood how the most trifling circumstances or characteristics have given rise to surnames which have been borne with pride for generation after generation for a thousand years or more, and yet many of them in their original significance were extremely undignified, not to say ludicrous.

It appears to be almost futile to search for a correct spelling of a surname of more than one syllable. All of them came into existence during the middle ages and their bearers, in the main, could neither read nor write. The spelling of surnames in records several centuries old was simply an *attempt* of scribes and conveyancers to spell names. Signatures are helpful, but those of the same surname differ from each other, and it has often happened that a person spelled his surname different ways in signing different documents. Even when the exact linguistic derivation can be determined, it will be found that the stem and its prefixes or suffixes, which entered into the composition of a name, have changed with time.

However, it may be of interest to those bearing the name of Ficklin in its various forms, to know what has been ascertained regarding its history.

The name appears in three forms in America: Ficklin, Ficklen, and Fickling. The descendants of the two oldest sons of the Virginia immigrant, William and Thomas, who live largely in Middle West and West, spell the name Ficklin, as do the descendants of Anthony, living in Virginia. The descendants of Benjamin, the youngest son of the immigrant, who reside mainly in Virginia and Kentucky, spell the name Ficklen. It will be noted in the next chapter that the name of the immigrant is spelled in old records, from 1736 to 1756, both as Ficklin and Fickling. William and Thomas, sons of the immigrant, signed their names Ficklen to a deed dated 1756 and published elsewhere in this volume. William subsequently, in various deeds on record in Spottsylvania, signed his name Fick*lin*, as likewise did Thomas in his will, dated 1778. Anthony continued to sign his name Fick*len*, as shown by deed in Stafford, dated 1784. There is no document known to which Benjamin, youngest son of the immigrant, signed his name. In the Virginia census of 1785 his name and that of his brother, Anthony, appears as Fick*len*, and in the record of the appraisement of his estate (Stafford, 1805) his name is spelled Fick*len*.

The descendants of the South Carolina immigrant, who reside largely in the Carolinas and the Gulf states, spell the name Fick*ling*, as do most of those of the name living in England at the present time.

It is needless to say that every possible other variation in the spelling of the name appears in old records in England—for instance, Fokelyn, Fickellen, Ficklinge, Fiklinge, Ficilinge, Ficlin, Ficklyn, Fitlin, Fitling, Fittlinge. (No distinction need be made between Ficling and Fitling, for in the old writing it is at times impossible to say whether a "c" or a "t" is intended, the two letters being practically identical.) It will be noted, in the article of Walter Rye, that Fickelyn is the way the name appears in the oldest known record, about 1279.

It was a common practice in the middle ages, and even later times, to write "ff" for capital F. This continues in some families to the present day, and arose from the old way of writing the middle cross of F, which made the letter resemble two small f's. In this connection, these excerpts from the old church register at Twyford, Norfolk, will be of interest:

"Willmus fficklyn filius Gwalteri fficklyn and Alicia Uxoris ejus baptizatus fuit tertio die Marcij, 1582."

"Ales the wife of Mathew ffiklinge was buried XXII day of March Ano Dni, 1599. P. Me Henr Hilton Rector ibim."

Those who have studied the name agree very generally that it is of Saxon origin. The name is evidently a diminutive, for the Saxon termination *ling* or its contractions signify "young of" or "son of." There are two parishes called "Ling," in Somerset and Norfolk, and it may be that a surname ending in "ling" might have been adopted by a person living in one of these parishes. This termination was added to the name "Fick" or "Fyke," "Vick," "Vik," or "Wicke," or some similar name—the V and W in old Germanic languages being pronounced in a similar manner to the English F.

Mr. Harry C. Ficklen, of Danville, Virginia, has given much intelligent

study to the origin of his surname, and the writer believes he has presented by
far the most plausible account of its origin, and hence publishes below a very
able paper prepared by him on that subject:

"The origin of a surname such as 'Ficklen,' 'Ficklin,' or 'Fickling,' must
always, within certain limits, be more or less conjectural, because (1st) it may
be a corruption from some other word or spelling which in the lapse of time has
become hopelessly disguised, and (2nd) if the original 'root' or 'substantive
idea' of the name is discoverable or patent, the true significance may depend
entirely upon either a primary or secondary meaning of the 'root' word—and
the primary and secondary meanings are often far apart—possibly and curious-
ly enough, even antonyms; that is to say, the significance of a descriptive surname will often depend upon whether its assumption or bestowal was synchron-
ous with a primary or with a secondary meaning, and the meaning of a proper
name as derived from a common noun may be a question of the antiquity of the
appellative.

"In the name before us—'Ficklen' or 'Ficklin'—the second syllable is
clearly the suffix seen in so many proper and common nouns and is the equiva-
lent of that '*ling*' which is seen in such surnames as 'Kipling' and in such common nouns as 'duckling.' It may roughly be defined as meaning 'off-spring
of.' Both 'ling' and 'ing' are 'derivatives' having the effect of a post-positive
'Mc' or 'Mac' ('son of').

"The 'root' or 'substantive idea' of '*Ficklin*' is '*Fick*' or rather '*fic*,' for
'k' after hard 'c' in English orthography is purely typographical, or perhaps I
should say, 'autographical'; that is to say, the 'k' is entirely a parenthetical
notation to show that the 'c' is sounded hard like 'k' and not soft like 's.'
(When many of the early scribes wrote hard 'c' as in 'music,' to be distin-
guished from soft 'c' in 'musician,' they posted the ignorant by writing, by way
of memento, '*music(k)*,' and then there came along copying blunderers who
could not make fine distinctions and made the parenthetical notation a part of
the word's spelling—manuscripts became as binding as law precedents, and
when printing presses, without learning [for philological study is very modern],
suddenly crystallized English spelling, we found ourselves with a large number
of words having the redundant '*ck*'—and later philological quidnuncs have
been chopping off final 'k's' ever since—not always wisely, for there is often
much philosophy and utility in '*ck*,' seeing that 'c' is so variable, and yet for

other high reasons is not always interchangeable with 'k'). The above root 'fic' is probably traceable to the root of a Middle English verb 'fiken,' which means 'to feign,' 'to dissemble,' etc., and this is derived from the Anglo-Saxon root 'fic' in 'fician,' or 'be-fician,' a verb meaning 'to deceive' or 'use craft'— the same root as that of the Anglo-Saxon adjective 'ficol,' which means 'crafty' —a fine illustration of the difference between primary and secondary meanings —for the Anglo-Saxon 'ficol' is the prototype of our present 'fickle.' Whether there was ever any patriarch of this modern name who in the rude old Saxon times, when 'he who wills may take and he may keep who can,' had fastened upon him by his fellows and 'nigh-boors' the descriptive epithet of 'the crafty one'—*Fic* or *Fick*—we may not know, but indications point to that conclusion. If the conclusion be correct, the origin of the surname is anything but odious. The imputation of craftiness in such primitive times has by no means the implications of such a 'nick-name,' as it were, of to-day. For instance, a progenitor barbarian of the German forest would be a marked or noted man, when it came to nomenclature, for just such a trait as craftiness, wariness, even deceitfulness; and what we, 'heirs of all the ages' and a slowly evolved racial civilization, would single out as a high moral characteristic would stamp, and probably doom, its exemplar of primitive times as a weakling.

"Just as the 'historical estimate' is a projecting of the mind or judgment into an attitude of contemporary contemplation—a judging of men and events by their times, so it is in the rise of surnames. An ascription of craftiness by one's primitive neighbors was a marking from positive mental characteristics— far more noteworthy by the 'historical method' than any naming from places or other accidents or trifling peculiarities. It is as if 'mother-wit' and positive character controlled the naming. The 'astuteness' of racial civilization—the 'long result of time'—is the 'craftiness' which marked the primitive progenitor. 'Nobody ever called us fools' is frequently an expression of family pride with many to-day.

"There survives in the Yorkshire dialect to-day the intransitive verb 'fick,' 'to struggle,' 'to kick,' and this is a dialectal variation of the noun and verb 'fike' (vowel pronunciation as in 'pike,' though the vowel is said to be, properly, short—hence the variations 'fick' and 'fyke'), which survives to-day only in Scotch and Provincial English, and signifies 'restlessness' and 'to move about in a quick, uneasy way,' 'be constantly in motion,' etc. This word has cognate forms in Icelandic and the Norse languages with various meanings such as 'to hunt after,' 'to strive,' 'to take trouble,' etc. And if the modern surname in question had its origin directly from such a form as '*fick*,' mentioned last above, then it might be interpreted as 'the tribe of strugglers' (in the various meanings of that term), with sidelights of probable meaning coming from the cognate forms quoted above. (It is to be remembered that a characterization which grew into a surname may originally have been applied to a whole group of kindred and does not always predicate some single progenitor, no matter if a part of the surname is a suffix of origin.)

"The Provincial English word *fick* or *fike*, as last set forth above, is believed to have had its origin in, or to be a secondary use of, the older word '*fike*' (now obsolete) derived from the Middle English infinitive '*fiken*,' first mentioned above, which in turn is derived from the Anglo-Saxon infinitive '*fician*' or 'be-fician' (root = '*fic*') which has for its root-idea 'craftiness,' as aforesaid. So, while two words spelled 'fike,' having different meanings, exist, it is more logical to go back to the older form in seeking our probable derivation, and this is probably not inaccurately described as one of the Anglo-Saxon forms which show Norse influence.

"That the root and root-idea of this modern surname is '*fic*,' that is, that it is not much of a corruption from anything else—and that it runs back in to a broadly Saxon genesis, is rendered plausible by the existence of Fick as a German surname of to-day (as witness the 19th century scholars Adolf Fick, physiologist, and August Fick, philologist).

"It is to be noted also that the 'l' in this surname may be the 'l' in the Anglo-Saxon adjective 'ficol,' 'crafty,' plus the derivative termination 'ing,' the whole compound finally corrupting into a present form.

"Notwithstanding all that has been said, it is entirely possible that the name '*Fickling*' may be simply a form of the word 'viking.' which is a composite of *vik*, 'a bay' and the suffix 'ing' denoting origin (vikings = 'bay men'). In all Germanic tongues 'f' and 'v' are often the same consonant, as it were, 'f' being rather a descendant of 'v.' The suffix 'ling' is really a compound suffix, 'ing' being the real root. It is probable that 'ing' was attached to so many roots ending in 'l,' which in primitive chirography was often doubled, that language-blunderers, who are potent language-makers, attached to 'ing' (as a suffix of origin) something that was no integral part of it—until finally 'ling' became as much the derivative suffix as 'ing,' and the two forms ran parallel. (Carelessness of speech and lazy vocalization are not merely modern factors in language-wrecking or language-making.)

"Therefore '*vik-ling*'—easily turning into '*fik-ling*' or 'Fickling'—would be an Anglo-Saxon or Early or Middle English attempt to produce a form having the meaning of the modern word 'viking'—'a man of the bay'—a piratical rover, such as every individual of the finally colonizing Norsemen was. Once get an 'l' following the root 'vik,' and our own vocal organs of to-day will make it plain how easily an initial sonant 'v' will be assimilated into the surd 'f.' To support this last surmise we have the fact that 'viking' is an imported, late, or 'literary' word entirely. We may, therefore, suppose a patronymic to have grown out of its root with the derivative 'ling,' in the manner indicated, without doing violence to the history of linguistic habit or tendency.

"To sum up, it would be a reasonable philological 'guess' that the primitive band of kindred who came into an appellation which we now have in the patronymic of Ficklen, Ficklin, or Fickling, were 'crafty ones' or some of the 'bay men' known as vikings; and from a philological standpoint the genesis is as respectable, poetical, and inspiring as could be wished."

CHAPTER VII.

___

THE FIRST OF THE FICKLINS IN VIRGINIA.

___

A large number of publications showing lists of immigrants to, and early settlers of, nearly every American colony has been searched, but the name of Ficklin is not mentioned. However, many whose names appear in Hotten's Lists of Immigrants (J. W. Bouton, New York, publisher), for instance, were deported or banished from the mother country, and the fact that no member of the family is mentioned in any such list allows us to conclude that those who did immigrate to America paid their passage like self-respecting men and women. A kinsman of the writer made a search of the records in London with a view to tracing the sailing of any Ficklin from that port, but with no success.

The first mention of the name in old records in Virginia is in a deed of lease from Scarlet Hancock to John Tayloe, dated 1736, and recorded in King George county, and reading in part as follows:

"The lease made to John Gilbert for his and his wife's life, reserving no rent, and to William Ficklin for fourteen years, paying rent, are to have their full effect, anything in this deed to the contrary or seeming to the contrary notwithstanding."

The above statement shows that Scarlet Hancock had previously leased part of this land to William Ficklin for a period of fourteen years, but it does not give the date of the prior lease. No record of this lease from Hancock to Ficklin can be found either in King George or the older county of Richmond, of which King George was once a part. That such a document existed there can be no doubt, and the date it bore will be determined below.

In a deed of re-lease from said Hancock to said Tayloe, dated 26 March, 1736, and likewise recorded, will be noted:

"* * * That the said Scarlet Hancock * * * hath bargained and sold * * * unto the said John Tayloe all that piece or parcel of land containing three hundred thirty-seven and one-half acres, situated * * * in the Parish of Brunswick, in the County of King George, upon the Rappahannock river, on the north side thereof, being the land whereon John Gilbert and William Fickling now live. * * * Bounded as followeth (viz.): Beginning at an ash tree at the north of a branch by a great piece of sunken grounds upon the river side, which ash is the corner tree of Richard Shipnay, and extending into the woods by a line of marked trees N. 15° west seven hundred and twelve perches to a scrubby red oak, thence west northwest fifty-nine perches by a white oak on the west side of a path leading to Parson Waugh's, thence ten degrees by a half east intersecting the said path divers times, by a line of marked trees seven hundred and fifteen perches to a chestnut oak standing in the sunken ground aforesaid, which said land divides the land hereby granted from the land of * * * John Fossaker, and from the said chestnut oak one hundred and seven perches to the first mentioned ash tree. * * *"

Likewise recorded in the same county is a deed of lease from the above mentioned John Tayloe to William Ficklin and wife, Sarah, of the Parish of Brunswick and county of King George, dated 27 May, 1745, from which the following is taken:

"In consideration of the yearly rents * * * which on the part of William Ficklin are paid * * * doth demise, grant, and farm lett unto the said William Ficklin one messuage or tenement scituate lying and being in the Parish of Brunswick and County of King George now in the possession of the said Ficklin by lease from Scarlet Hancock of whom the said Tayloe purchased by estimation one hundred and fifty acres being part of that tract of land whereon John Gilbert now lives * * * to have and to hold said premises and tenement hereby demised unto said Ficklin and Sarah, his wife, or to the longest liver of them yielding and paying therefor yearly * * * the yearly rent of eight hundred pounds of good and lawful tobacco or cash * * * together with the quitrents due unto the Lord Proprietor, and the said William Ficklin and Sarah his wife yearly during the natural life of them or either of them shall and will pay unto said Tayloe * * *"

Since this lease of 1745 was evidently a renewal of the lease from Scarlet Hancock to William Ficklin, which lease was mentioned in the two earlier documents also, and since that lease was for fourteen years, the agreement must have been entered into fourteen years prior to 1745, or in 1731. It is not at all likely that William Ficklin would have leased a tract of ground for as long a term as fourteen years unless he had previously resided in that region for several years and was thoroughly acquainted with the possibilities of the land he was leasing. It is safe, therefore, to conclude that he was living in Virginia in 1725 or earlier, perhaps on the same land thus leased and which in 1745 he leased for life.

There is also of record in King George a deed of gift (alluded to in the preface of this volume), which has such an important bearing on the genealogical history of the family that it is published in full herewith:

"To ALL CHRISTIAN PEOPLE to whom this Present Writing shall come. We, Sarah Fickling (Widow and Relict of William Fickling late of the County of King George Deceased), Ignatious West and Patience his wife, Stephen Bowen and Sarah his wife, Robert Roach and Elizabeth his wife, William Fickling, Thomas Fickling and Anthony Fickling, of the County of King George

"SEND GREETING KNOW YE that we the said Sarah Fickling, Ignatious West and Patience his wife, Stephen Bowen and Sarah his wife, Robert Roach and Elizabeth his wife, William Fickling, Thomas Fickling, and Anthony Fickling for and in consideration of the natural love and affection which we and each of us have and bear unto our beloved Brother *Benjamin Fickling of the said County, youngest child of the said William Fickling deceased, as well for his advancement in the world as for divers other good causes and considerations us thereunto moving have and each of us hath given and granted and by these presents do and each of them doth give and grant unto the said Benjamin Fickling all and singular our and each of our Respective Parts Proportions Shares or Rights which we or any or either of us both shall or may have of or in any part or parcel of all and singular the goods and chattels rights and credits whatsoever which were of the said William Fick (sic) Deced. at the time of his decease in whose hands custody or possession the same can or may be found. To have hold and enjoy all and singular the goods chattels

---

*(The conveyancer who wrote the above deed for its signers was undoubtedly a careless one, as he makes Sarah Fickling, widow and relict of William Fickling, speak of said William Fickling's youngest child, Benjamin, as "our brother" in a deed in which said Benjamin's brothers and sisters were joining her. There can be no doubt, however, I think, from the paper he drew, what the relationship of the parties was. I take it that Sarah was the mother of Patience West, Sarah Bowen, Elizabeth Roach, and of William, Thomas and Anthony Fickling, who sign the deed.—Note of comment by H. C. Ficklen, of Danville, Va.)

and personal estate aforesaid unto the said Benjamin Fickling his Heirs Executors administrators and assigns To the only proper use benefit and behoof of him the said Benjamin Fickling his heirs executors administrators and assigns forever and we the said Sarah Fickling, Ignatious West and Patience his wife, Stephen Bowen and Sarah his wife, Robert Roach and Elizabeth his wife, William Fickling, Thomas Fickling, and Anthony Fickling all and singular the aforesaid goods chattels and premises unto the said Benjamin Fickling his heirs executors administrators and assigns against all persons whatsoever shall and will warrant and forever defend by these presents. In Witness whereof the parties to this present writing hath interchangeably set their hands and seals this second day of November one thousand seven hundred and fifty-six and in the Thirtieth year of the reign of our Sovereign Lord King George the Second.†

her
SARAH FICKLING (Seal)
mark

IGNATIOUS WEST (Seal)

her
PATIENCE WEST (Seal)
mark

STEPHEN BOWEN (Seal)

her
SARAH BOWEN (Seal)
mark

his
ROBERT ROACH (Seal)
mark

her
ELIZABETH ROACH (Seal)
mark

WILLIAM FICKLEN (Seal)

THOMAS FICKLEN (Seal)

his
ANTHONY FICKLEN (Seal)
mark

†It will be of interest to compare the list of Christian names of the first Ficklin family in Virginia with those which appear in the will of Benjamin ffitling of Bedingham, Norfolk, dated 1708. (Registered at the Probate office, H. M. High Court of Justice, The Close, Norwich.) His heirs were as follows: wife, Elizabeth; younger children, Robert and Sarah ffitling; John ffitling; William ffitling; Mary, wife of Jeremiah ffitling; and Elizabeth, wife of William Andrews. This will reveals, however, no relationship to the Ficklins in Virginia other than that suggested in the similarity of names.

"Sealed and acknowledged in the presence of
> WILLIAM BOWEN
> STEPHEN HANSFORD
> GERARD BANKS

"At a court held for King George County the 7th. day of April, 1757, this deed of Gift from under the hands and seals of Sarah Fickling and the others thereto subscribed to Benjamin Fickling was proved by the oaths of William Bowen, Stephen Hansford and Gerard Banks and ordered to be recorded and is truly recorded.

Test.   ROB. ARMISTEAD, Co. Cler.

"State of Virginia,
"County of King George, to-wit:

"I, F. C. S. Hunter, Clerk of the Circuit Court for the County aforesaid, in the State of Virginia, do hereby certify that the foregoing is a true copy of a deed from Sarah Fickling *et als* to Benjamin Fickling, as appears in the records of my said office.

"Given under my hand this 30th. day of December, 1909.

"F. C. S. HUNTER, Clerk."

Fortunately William Slaughter, in his manuscript of 1860, and also Slaughter W. Ficklin in his pamphlet of 1870, which was founded on the said manuscript, preserve, as handed down, a bit of family history which goes far to prove that the William Ficklin mentioned so often in the documents quoted in this chapter, was the Ficklin immigrant to Virginia. This account, however, was transmitted from one generation to another for over a century, but apparently never recorded till 1860. As a result, the name *Benjamin*, for generations a name in the Ficklin family, was substituted for *William*, the Christian name of the immigrant. No *Benjamin* Ficklin is mentioned in the records of King George, excepting the one mentioned in the deed of gift, published above, and he is therein shown to have been a son of *William* Ficklin and Sarah, his wife. The following is taken from the pamphlet mentioned:

"The first of the Ficklins in Virginia was Benjamin, who came from England when a young man and settled in King George. A brother named

George* sailed with Benjamin, but stopped at Bermuda. It is believed he afterwards went to South Carolina, and that he is ancestor of the families of that name in that quarter who add 'g' to their names, writing it Fickling, using 'i' instead of 'e.' Benjamin was the ancestor of all the families living in Virginia and of those who removed from there. * * * From the best data that can be obtained, it is quite safe to say that the arrival of Benjamin Ficklin in the Colony of Virginia was about 1720 or 1730. Benjamin had four sons who married and settled in Virginia, William, Thomas, Anthony and Benjamin."

These four sons, it will be noted, are mentioned in the same order of age in the deed of gift of 1756, and are shown therein to have been the sons of *William* and not of Benjamin. William and Sarah appear as Christian names in every branch of the family to this day. The oldest son of the immigrant was also named William. Thomas Ficklin of King George, whom every account of the family names as a son of the immigrant, identifies himself, in his will (1778), as the son of William and Sarah Ficklin, for he mentions his brother, Benjamin, and nephew, James Bowen. Reference to the deed will show that the Thomas mentioned therein had a brother, Benjamin, and a sister, Sarah, who married a Bowen. Neither the Slaughter manuscript nor the pamphlet of Slaughter W. Ficklin mention any daughters of the immigrant. The old deed explains traditions which exist allying by intermarriage the Ficklin, Bowen and West families.

There is a tradition to the effect that the Ficklin immigrant married a sister of Henry Fielding, the English writer. The name Fielding appears as a Christian name in every generation of the descendants of Benjamin Ficklen, youngest son of the immigrant, and would indicate that the Ficklens and Fieldings might be allied by intermarriage. The immigrant's wife, Sarah, may have been a Fielding, or his son, Benjamin, may have married a Fielding, for nothing has been learned concerning the latter's wife. Henry Fielding had

---

*Unfortunately no trace has been found of this George Fickling who is supposed to have been a brother of the Ficklin of Virginia and to have settled in South Carolina. That a Fickling did settle there about 1720 or 1730 there can be no doubt, for there have been numerous families of that name in that region for more than a century. All the records of Colleton and Beaufort counties, where the first families of that name in that colony lived, were wantonly destroyed by General Sherman's troops in 1865. The records of the State Land office contain the earliest mention of the name in a grant of a small tract of land (38 acres) in Colleton county to *Jeremiah* Fickling, 4 May, 1752. The first mention of a *George* Fickling is in the returns for Colleton county at the census of 1790. An effort has been made to have the records of the Bermuda Islands examined, since so many of the immigrants to the American colonies touched or tarried there, but no reply could be obtained from any official at Hamilton, the capital.

three sisters, one of whom was named Sarah, but all of them died unmarried (Nichol's History of Leicestershire, 1795). If either Ficklin married a Fielding, he probably married one of the Virginia Fieldings, but no record of such marriage has been found.

Tradition has it also that the Ficklins in Virginia held for a number of years a grant of land from George II, King of England. Such grant, if made at all, would have been made to the Ficklin immigrant, for George II died in 1760. Of all grants, those from the King would have been most faithfully recorded in the Colonial Land office. The old deeds quoted above show that William Ficklin lived on leased land. The following letter bears on this point:

"Commonwealth of Virginia,
    Land Office,

"Richmond, Va., Feby. 5th, 1909.

"W. H. Ficklin, Esq.,
    University Park, Colo.

"Dear Sir:

    "Replying to your letter of the 3rd inst. I have made an examination of the records of King George County, also of records covering entire state covering a period from 1623 to 1780 and do not find record of the name Ficklin appearing thereon. It is possible that they purchased their land from a private party, then, that would only be of record in the county in which the land was situated. This you could find by a search of the records of King George County.   Yours very truly,

"JOHN W. RICHARDSON, Register."

The approximate age of William Ficklin may be arrived at as follows: John Ficklin, son of the second William, was born in 1755 (from John Ficklin's application for pension in U. S. Pension office). John's older brother, Thomas, was the head of a family in 1772 (Spottsylvania records— deed from Spottswood to Ficklin, 15 Sept., 1772) and was probably born about 1750. The second William, father of these, must have been born about 1728. But this William was not the oldest child, as shown by the deed of 1756. He was the fourth child. His oldest sister, Patience, was born about 1722. William Slaughter states that the immigrant came to Virginia when a young man. He therefore was born about 1690 or 1700. If he arrived in Virginia about 1720 or 1730, as believed, he was already married or married very shortly after his arrival. He was about sixty years of age when he died in 1756.

Among the friends and neighbors of the first Ficklin family in Virginia, who are mentioned in the old documents, and with several of which families the Ficklins intermarried, were the Bruces, Bankses, Corbins, Bowens, Fewells, Fitzhughs, Gilberts, Grants, Hansfords, Schilcottes, Taliaferros, and Thorntons.

To sum up: William Ficklin and perhaps his wife, Sarah, arrived in Virginia about 1720 or 1730, and settled on about one hundred and fifty acres of leased land on the north bank of the Rappahannock river, in Brunswick parish, King George county. Here they spent the remainder of their lives. Tobacco was the chief product of their farm and out of this they were allowed to pay their rent, for at that time, tobacco was currency. Here they reared a family of seven children, three daughters and four sons, all of whom lived to manhood or womanhood. William Ficklin died in 1756, when about sixty years of age. He probably died suddenly, since the deed of 1756 indicates that he left no will. All his children, excepting his two youngest sons, were married by this time and he had several grand-children. His widow survived him and doubtless continued to reside on the old plantation on the Rappahannock, for they had leased it for the remainder of their lives, but of her there is no further record.

At this time gentlemen, when in full dress, wore three-cornered cocked hats, long velvet coats, lace ruffles at their wrists, knee breeches, white silk stockings, and shoes with silver buckles. They kept their hair long, powdered it white, and tied it back in a twist or a queue with a black silk ribbon. Ladies wore gowns of brocade and rich silk almost stiff enough to stand alone. They also powdered their hair, so that all people of fashion, whether young or old, looked stately and venerable.

The gravestones in two old churchyards in Brunswick parish and one in St. Paul's, all in King George, have been examined* with a view to identifying the graves of any of this first family of Ficklins. The name does not appear, however, on any of the stones. There are many unmarked graves in these

*This examination was made by Miss Sallie P. Taliaferro and Messrs. Hunter and Wishart Taliaferro, all of Passapatanzy, King George Co., Va.

churchyards and they may have been buried in some of these. Mrs. S. M. Hardesty, of Washington, D. C., sister of Slaughter W. Ficklin, and one of the oldest of the family now living, writes that the land of the Ficklin immigrant was about twelve miles from Fredericksburg. In which case Lamb's Creek church, erected in 1717, still standing and in use, was nearest the Ficklin land. Muddy Creek church, in the same parish (Brunswick), was a few miles further away and is now in ruins. The first register of this parish was lost about a century ago, but since none of the family are mentioned in the first registers of the adjoining parishes of St. Paul's (King George) and Overwharton, 1720-1760 (Stafford), it is safe to conclude that William Ficklin and family worshipped frequently, if not regularly, at the nearest church, old Lamb's Creek.

CHAPTER VIII.

DESCENDANTS OF WILLIAM FICKLIN AND WIFE, SARAH, OF KING GEORGE COUNTY, VIRGINIA.

(In the following pages the name of each descendant appears twice as a rule—once as a *descendant*, in the right-hand column, numbered, and further on the name may again be found by following the left-hand column till the same number, in its right succession, is found among the *heads of families*. Names which will appear a second time are indicated by a star. Any descendant, having difficulty using this system of numbers, is urged to identify the name of some ancestor in the index, ascertain the number, and work backward and forward from this.)

1. William Ficklin (I) and wife, Sarah, reared three daughters and four sons as follows (see deed of 1756, published in preceding chapter):
    2. Patience, who married Ignatius West.
    3. Sarah, who married Stephen Bowen, and had a son, James.
    4. Elizabeth, who married Robert Roach.
    *5. William (II).
    *6. Thomas (I).
    *7. Anthony.
    *8. Benjamin (I).

5. William Ficklin (II), son of William (I) and Sarah Ficklin, was born in King George about 1728. He settled on a farm on the Rappahannock river, in St. George's parish, Spottsylvania county, near Fredericksburg. This farm adjoined that of the Reverend James Marye, and was probably a part of the battlefield of Fredericksburg. William Ficklin's name appears on the county records from 1759 to 1789. His wife, whose name has not been learned, probably died in early life, since she is not mentioned

at all in any deed to or from her husband.   The date of his death is not known and no record of his will has been found.   He had one daughter, concerning whom nothing is known (Slaughter MS.)†, and four sons:

    *9. Thomas.
    *10. John.
    *11. Joseph.
    *12. Charles.

6. Thomas Ficklin (I), son of William (I) and Sarah Ficklin, lived all his life in King George county.   He married Susannah Bruce, daughter of Charles Bruce of King George (will of Ch. Bruce, King George, 1754). ‡Thomas Ficklin doubtless survived his wife, as he does not mention her in his will, proved 3 December, 1778.   His children, named in the will, were as follows:

    13. Susannah, who married Wm. Sweetnaim.
    14. Ann, who married a Fewell.
    15. Margaret, who married Wm. Jenkins.
    16. Sarah, who married John Swetnam, and had son, John Swetnam, Jr., whose daughter, Sarah Ficklin Swetnam, married a Bryan and lives at Stafford C. H., Va.
    17. Elizabeth.
    18. Lucy.
    *19. John.

(One daughter of Thomas Ficklin married a Duff, and moved to Kentucky.   Another married a Matthews, and died in Virginia [Slaughter MS.].   One daughter, not mentioned in the will, doubtless died before the will was made.   She married a Bell, for the will mentions a grandson, Lewis Bell.)

7. Anthony Ficklen, son of William (I) and Sarah Ficklin, was born in King George county, and resided at Poplar Settlement in Stafford county,

---

†There was an Ester Ficklin who was witness to the will of Jarvis Haydon of Spottsylvania Co., 10 September, 1788, who is not accounted for in this volume. She may have been the daughter of William, but it is more probable that she was Easter Ficklin (nee Newby), wife of Joseph (No. 11), son of William.

‡Following is an extract from a letter of Judge P. W. Strother, of Pearisburg, Va., to Mrs. Nancy P. Ballard, Chatham, Va., dated 8 November, 1896: "In April, 1754, will of Charles Bruce, probated, devises to his sons, William and Charles, and to five daughters, Susannah Ficklen, wife of Thomas F., Elizabeth Bruce, Mary, Frances, etc. * * *"

about ten miles from Falmouth (Slaughter MS.). He married Elizabeth Bruce, daughter of Ch. Bruce of King George, whose wife is supposed to have been a Pannill (Virginia Hist. Mag., vol. 12, p. 452).† His name appears among the heads of families in the Virginia census of 1785 (Stafford county) in which the following is noted concerning him: "Anthony Ficklen, white souls 4, dwellings 1, other buildings 2." This is the last record of him. He died prior to 1810, since his name does not appear in the returns for Stafford county at that census. He mentions son, Charles, in deed signed by him, 1784. The names of his other children are taken from Slaughter MS.

    *20. Charles.
    *21. Benjamin.
    *22. Lewis.
    23. Frances, who married a Duncan, and left no issue.
    24. Elizabeth, who married a Stewart; their son and daughter went to Missouri.
    25. Mildred, who did not marry.
    26. Susan, who married a Bell and, after his death, went to Missouri with her family.

8. Benjamin Ficklen (I), youngest son of William (I) and Sarah Ficklin, was born in King George county, and resided at Poplar Settlement in Stafford county, near his brother, Anthony (Slaughter MS.). The deed of 1756 would indicate that he was a minor child at that time. His second son, Daniel, was born 26 March, 1766 (Family Bible of Daniel Ficklen). Benjamin was born about 1740. The name of his wife has not been learned.‡ The Virginia census 1785 (Stafford county) mentions him as follows: "Benjamin Ficklen, white souls 7, dwellings 1, other buildings 2." He must have died in 1805, as his estate was administered in that year (Stafford records). His children were as follows

†The will of Ch. Bruce (King George), 1754, indicates that his daughter Elizabeth, was single at that time. The will of Margaret Bruce, sister of Elizabeth (Spottsylvania, 1765), mentions Elizabeth as Elizabeth *Bronaugh*.
‡It is thought by some that the wife of this Benjamin may have been a Burwell, since that name appears frequently as a Christian name among his descendants. Mr. Geo. H. Burwell, of Millwood, Va., who has in his possession records of the Burwells, writes that he can find no instance of a marriage of a Ficklin and a Burwell.

(Slaughter MS. and Slaughter W. Ficklin's pamphlet of 1870, order of age not clearly shown) :

    *27. Fielding (I).
    *28. Daniel (I).
    *29. William.
    *30. Benjamin (II).
    *31. Mary.
    *32. Susan.
    *33. Elizabeth.
    *34. Sarah.

---

9. Thomas Ficklin, son of William (II), was born about 1750. He married Mary Herndon and resided in Spottsylvania county, where probably nearly all his children were born, till about 1780, when he emigrated to Kentucky. He and his wife and at least two of his children, Joseph and Philadelphia, were in the stockade at Bryant's Station, near Lexington, during the memorable siege of that place by a horde of more than five hundred savages led by the renegade, Simon Girty, August 15, 16 and 17, 1782. There were about ninety people in the stockade, counting all. Mary Herndon Ficklin and her little daughter, Philadelphia, were among the score of unarmed women and girls who ventured out of the stockade on the perilous mission of procuring water from a spring nearby—a deed of heroism rarely equaled in the annals of history. The writer of this volume, when a child in school, listened to an account of this siege, but little dreamed that some of his people were participants. But for this water the stockade, which was built of logs and dry as tinder at the time, would have been destroyed by the burning arrows, and the occupants massacred. While the men fought off the assailants, the women and children were busily occupied putting out fires. For a detailed account of this siege and the massacre at Blue Licks, two days later, where many who defended the stockade were slain, the reader is referred to volume twelve of the publications of The Filson Club of Louisville. The Lexington Chapter, Daughters of the American Revolution, recently erected a monument at the spring in commemoration of the heroism of the women and girls during the siege.

The census of 1810 shows that Thomas Ficklin was living in Scott county at that time.   The old records of that county have been destroyed and much that they would doubtless have revealed concerning him and his children has been lost.   The date of his death is not known, though his estate was administered in that county.   His children were (see Slaughter MS., Deed, Spottswood to Ficklin, Spottsylvania Co., Va., 15 Sept., 1772, and Filson Club publications, vol. 12) :

    *35.   John Herndon.

    *36.   Joseph.

    *37.   William Augustus.

    38.   Philadelphia, who was one of the children at Bryant's Station.   Nothing further known of her.

    39.   Margaret, who married a Piper and had daughter, Philadelphia, who married a Mitchell and lived near Scottville, Ky.

10. John Ficklin, son of William (II), was born in 1755.   He enlisted as a private from Spottsylvania Co. in Capt. Wm. Taliaferro's company, Col. Wm. Woodford's Virginia Troops, in September, 1775, and was mustered out at Williamsburg, in September, 1776.   He participated in the Battle of Great Bridge, 9 Dec., 1775.†   It is not known that he re-enlisted, but he was granted a pension late in life for his services (Survivors File, No. 35938, Rev. War, Bureau of Pensions).   He emigrated to Kentucky about 1780—probably with the great movement of Baptists from Spottsylvania and other counties in Virginia to Kentucky, about that time.   He settled on a farm in Liberty township, Jessamine county, near what is now the town of Keene.   This farm now belongs to Mrs. Fannie Cleveland, of Keene, Ky.   Mrs. Cleveland has preserved some old papers which once belonged to her great-grandfather, John Haydon, who settled in Jessamine, from Spottsylvania, about 1780.   Among these is a subscription list bearing the name of John Ficklin and others, amounts being in pounds and shillings—no date, but prior to the time of the adoption of a national currency in the United States, 1792.

Life in Kentucky at this time was a constant struggle with the wilderness and the redskin, and suggests the log cabin in the backwoods, flint

---

†An account of the Battle of Great Bridge may be found in Cooke's History of Virginia, p. 436.

and steel and tinder box, flint-lock rifle, coon-skin cap, and buck-skin jacket and breeches.

John Ficklin died 6 June, 1819, and is buried in an unmarked grave on his old farm. His wife, Mary, survived him and is buried beside him —her maiden name and the date of her death not known. The exact location of the graves is known, the remains of the log cabin are still to be seen, and the old spring runs as of yore.

Their children were as follows (from will of John Ficklin, proved August, 1819, Jessamine Co. records) :†

    *40. Jared, Jarrett, or Jarrot.
    41. Betsy, who married Hampton.
    *42. John.
    *43. William.
    *44. Thomas.
    45. Susan—nothing known of her.
    *46. Charles.
    47. Joel—nothing known of him.
    48. Catherine—nothing known of her.
    49. Price—nothing known of him.
    50. Sarah, who married Benjamin Payton, and had daughter, Patsy.

11. Joseph Ficklin, son of William (II), is thought to have emigrated to Kentucky with his brothers, Thomas and John. He was witness to a deed in Spottsylvania county, Va., in 1787. In 1797 the first party of settlers, in which were Joseph Ficklin, Tolliver Craig, and other pioneers, settled in Allen county at points east and north of the present site of Scottville (Collins' Hist. of Kentucky, vol. 2, p. 39). The following, concerning Joseph Ficklin, has been gleaned from letters written by Miss Louise Edmunds, of Willard, N. M., and Robert Ficklin Pulliam, of Scottville, Ky., both descendants of his. Joseph Ficklin married Easter

---

†"Jarrot" Ficklin was named executor of the will. Arrears of pension were paid to "Jarrett" Ficklin, exor., for Polly Ficklin, widow.

The following is an extract from a letter written by Orlando B. Ficklin, of Charleston, Ill., to Joseph Ficklin, of Columbia, Mo., 29 July, 1864: "Your grandfather, Jared Ficklin, was the first cousin of my father. Joseph Ficklin, of Lexington, was my uncle. He and myself, when I was a boy, spent a few days at Jared Ficklin's in what was then Mercer county, Kentucky. Your great-grandfather, John Ficklin, and my grandfather, Thomas Ficklin, were brothers, and used to visit each other, etc., * * *"

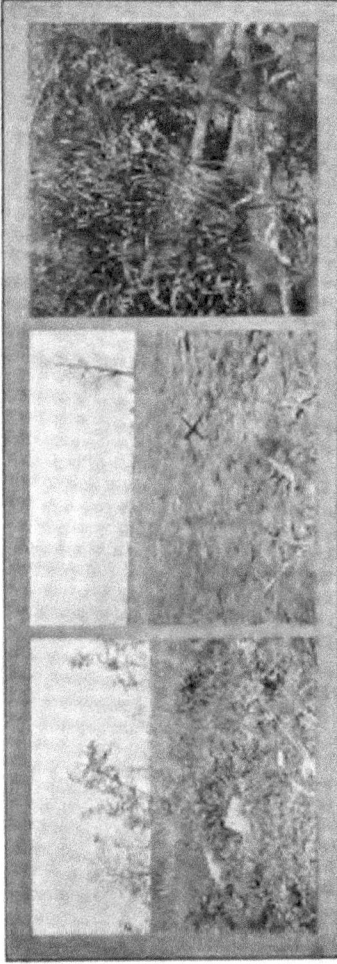

Scenes on old farm of John Ficklin in Jessamine County, Kentucky, taken by Mrs. Fannie Cleveland, present owner of the farm.

1. Remains of the old cabin which was erected about 1780.
2. Site of the graves of John Ficklin and wife, Mary—cross indicates exact location.
3. The spring near the old cabin.

Newby in Virginia. They resided on the old farm near Scottville the remainder of their lives and are buried there in unmarked graves. The dates of their deaths are not known. Joseph and his wife were Methodists, and, in their pioneer home, entertained Bishop Asbury, the first Methodist Bishop to visit America. The Bishop was very old, but often preached at their home, seated in an arm-chair, which had been placed on a dining-room table. Two children were born to Joseph and Easter Ficklin:

> 51. Robert, who married Kittie Coates, of Bowling Green, Ky., but died without issue. He is buried beside his father and mother on the old farm which now belongs to his namesake, Robert Ficklin Pulliam.
>
> *52. Margaret.

12. Charles Ficklin, son of William (II), came to an untimely end. The Slaughter manuscript states that "William had a son who died in Quebec"—first name not given. Even the name of this boy patriot, who gave his life for his country, and who was probably hastily buried by his comrades in a shallow trench in a foreign land, has been forgotten by his people. There is no monument to his memory unless it be in the fact that his name appears on the roster of the soldiers of the Revolution—a roll of honor on which any American citizen notes, with pride, the name of an ancestor or kinsman.

He enlisted for three years' service 23 December, 1776, in Capt. John Spottswood's Company, 10th Virginia Regiment, commanded by Colonel Edward Stevens. On the company muster roll for September, 1777, dated 9 October, 1777, he is reported as deceased (War Dept. records). Whether he died of wounds or disease is not known. At the time of his death, his regiment was engaged in the campaign against General Burgoyne and no doubt crossed the St. Lawrence into Quebec Province.

At a court held for Spottsylvania county, Virginia, 6 Sept., 1785, it being shown that Charles Ficklin served as a soldier in the Continental Army and died in the service, Thomas Ficklin† was declared to be his

---

†There is little probability that the Thomas, here named, was a son of Charles. Charles could not have been over twenty years old at the time of his death. Had he been married, his widow would have been made at least a joint heir to the land. The warrant was issued before Charles' nephew, Thomas, was born, and after his uncle, Thomas, died. The Thomas named as heir must have been Charles' brother, Thomas (No. 9).

heir (Order Book, 1782-1786). Warrant No. 3879, for one hundred acres of land, was issued from the Virginia land office 20 May, 1785, to Thomas Ficklin, heir at law of Charles Ficklin, who was entitled to the proportion of land allowed a private of the Continental Line for three years' service. _____

19. John Ficklin, son of Thomas (I), was born in King George county, Virginia, 8 May, 1762. He resided in this county till about 1790, when he moved to Fauquier. Meanwhile he married Judith Kenyon, born 3 Nov., 1772, daughter of James Kenyon, of Virginia, and niece of Lord Kenyon of England. The following is the wording of a church letter, which was issued them:

"John Ficklin and Judith Ficklin, the bearers, have been acceptable members of our Society in the Methodist Episcopal Church. Given under my hand this 2nd. day of September, 1798."

"CHADS CHALFFANT. "HEZEKIAH HARRIMAN, Stafford Circuit.

"BROTHER ROBERSON.

"JOHN JACOBS."

In deed, dated 10 Oct., 1798, John Ficklin mentions himself and wife, Judith, as citizens of Fauquier. They did not live long in Fauquier, for John Ficklin in his will, dated 30 Sept., 1803, speaks of himself as a citizen of Mason county, Kentucky, to which he had emigrated. He died 23 April, 1804, and his widow, 1 Nov., 1826. Both are buried on their old farm near Washington, Ky. In his will, John Ficklin provided for the emancipation of all his slaves. Their children, according to the will above mentioned, were as follows:†

    *53. Henry Kenyon.

    *54. Joseph Kenyon.

    *55. John Minton.

    *56. Lucy.

    *57. Thomas.

    *58. Judith Kenyon.

    *59. James Kenyon.

    *60. Robert.

_____

†Excepting where otherwise indicated, the data concerning John and Judith Ficklin and their descendants was gleaned largely from old family Bibles and papers by the late Miss Alice Ficklin, of Maysville, Ky., and her niece, Miss Anna C. Shackleford, of Chicago.

20. Charles Ficklin, son of Anthony, lived nearly all his life in Fauquier. His father speaks of him as a citizen of that county in a deed dated 29 Oct., 1784 (Stafford records). He speaks of himself as a citizen of Fauquier in his will, which was probated 28 Oct., 1816. His wife, Mary,† is mentioned in the will, and the children named therein were as follows:‡

    61. Anthony Strother, was living in Stafford in 1810 (Census). He married but died childless, 1844, in Fauquier, where his estate was administered.

    62. Charles B., never married.

    63. Betsy, did not marry—lived with her sister, Mrs. Tate.

    64. Susan B., married a Mr. Robinson, and lived at Wheeling, W. Va.

    65. Maria Pannell, married Maj. Thomas Tate and had one child, Mary Strother Tate, who married John W. Taylor, and reared six children: Maria Virginia, Sarah, Margaret, India Strother, Thomas Tate and Mary L.

    66. Nancy, who married Geo. Buckner Fant, 15 December, 1815, and emigrated to Missouri. They had a son, Charles Ficklin Fant. Miss M. E. Deatherage, of Carrollton, Mo., is a descendant of theirs.

    67. Drucilla Harriet, married Charles Montgomery Johnson and moved to Missouri. They had a son, Charles Ficklin Johnson, who died in St. Charles, Mo., 7 June, 1910.

    68. Polly, who married Philip Foushe.

21. Benjamin Ficklin, son of Anthony, married Susannah Foushee, in 1787. (Culpeper county marriage records.) This may have been his second

†The maiden name of Mary, wife of Charles Ficklin, has been handed down to her descendants as Mary Strother, daughter of Anthony Strother of Spottsylvania county. It will be noted her first child was named in honor of Anthony Strother, and she had a granddaughter named Mary Strother Tate. See, however, foot note under No. 21.

‡Data concerning the children of Charles and Mary Ficklin, other than that contained in the will, was gleaned from Slaughter W. Ficklin's pamphlet of 1870, and from letters written by Mrs. W. J. Hutchinson, Caspiana, La., Miss Sallie S. Fulton, Seven Mile Ford, Va., and Thomas T. Taylor, Broadford, Va.

marriage.† His name appears on the Stafford records as grantor and grantee in deeds dated 1809. In deed, dated 10 April, 1813, Benjamin Ficklen and wife, Susannah, convey land to Wm. R. Gordon. In this deed, Benjamin speaks of himself as a citizen of Stafford. The census returns for Stafford county, 1810, show that he and his wife were over forty-five years of age, and living with them were one white female (probably a daughter), over twenty-six and under forty-five, and two white males (probably sons), over sixteen and under twenty-six. They owned nineteen slaves at that time. Little is known of their children. Col. Theodore H. Ficklin, of Alexandria, Va., writes that his grandfather, Famous Ficklin, whose name appears on the records in Richmond county, was a son of this Benjamin.

*69. Famous Ficklin.

(There was a Cyrus Ficklin, of Culpeper county, who deeded property to Chas. Chilton, in 1832, and whose estate was administered in 1835, who is not accounted for in this volume. He probably belonged in this branch of the family and may have been a son of this Benjamin. The records concerning him mention no children nor other relatives.)

22. Lewis Ficklin, son of Anthony, lived first in Stafford, as shown by the census of 1810. He was then over twenty-six and under forty-five years of age. The returns would indicate that his wife was living and that he had two daughters and two sons. He had fourteen slaves at that time. There is a letter of attorney, of record in Stafford, dated 10 July, 1826, from Richard Simms to Lewis Ficklen. He was, however, probably living in Fauquier at that time, for his will was probated in that county in 1828, and his estate administered there in the years following. His wife was Sinphah Rosa Enfield Phillips, born 10 April, 1775 (Hayden's "Virginia Genealogies," p. 158; also Dinwiddie Genealogy, vol. 1). Their sons were:‡

†On p. 163, vol. 2, Southern Hist. Assn. Publications, is a statement that Mary Strother, born 2 June, 1757, daughter of Anthony Strother of Spottsylvania Co., and second wife, Mary James, married Benjamin Ficklin of Fauquier. This statement can apply to no other Benjamin than he who was son of Anthony. There is no record of a Benjamin Ficklin having ever lived in Fauquier. This Benjamin was a citizen of Stafford and married Susannah Foushee in 1787. He must have been at least fifty years of age when he and Susannah signed the deed of 1813.
See, also, footnote under No. 20.
‡Data concerning the descendants of Lewis and Enfield Ficklin was gleaned from Hayden's "Virginia Genealogies," and from letters from Miss Alice Dinwiddie Ficklin, of Bealeton, Va., and James W. Ficklin, of Warrenton, Va.

70. William Phillips, who lived in Fauquier county, where his name appears on the records as late as 1846. He married (1) Ann Martin, and (2) Frances Dulaney. Two sons were the result of the first union: (a) William Lewis, of Midland, Va., who served throughout the Civil War in the 4th Virginia Cavalry, paroled as lieutenant. He married Lucy, daughter of Col. Lawson Eastman, of Rappahannock Co., and had four sons and two daughters: William P., Claude, John and George, and Alice Dinwiddie and Annie; (b) John, who served in the same regiment as his brother, during the Civil War, and fell at the Battle of Travillian Station, near Richmond.

71. Gustavus, who married Virginia E. Nelson, of Fauquier, and reared one son, James W., of Warrenton, Va., who married (1) Miss Green, (2) Miss Jasper, and (3) Miss McDonald, and has a son Lewis Hamilton.

27. Fielding Ficklen (I), son of Benjamin (I), lived and died in Culpeper county, Virginia. He married Elizabeth Fant, 24 December, 1791, and died in 1809—a comparatively young man. His will is on record in Culpeper. His widow died in 1814. Both are buried near their old home in Culpeper. They had a handsome residence, which has since burned. Their children were as follows:†

*72. James Grant.
*73. George.
*74. Joseph Burwell.
*75. Fielding (II).
*76. Sarah.
*77. Harriet.
*78. Eliza.

†The data concerning Fielding Ficklen was gleaned from the Slaughter manuscript, and from letters written by Mrs. Kate Ficklen Marshall, of Lynchburg, Va., and H. C. Ficklen, of Danville, Va.

28. Daniel Ficklen (I), son of Benjamin (I), was born in Stafford county, Virginia, 26 March, 1766, emigrated to Fleming county, Kentucky, at an early age. 27 March, 1794, he married Delilah Leonard, daughter of Noble Leonard. Daniel Ficklen died 19 September, 1844. His wife died 19 April, 1851. Their old Bible, containing much information concerning his descendants, is in the possession of Mrs. Leila M. Ficklen, of Memphis. To this union eleven children were born:†

    *79.   Noble V.
    *80.   William.
    *81.   Malinda.
    *82.   Sarah.
    *83.   James L.
    *84.   Caroline. } Twins.
    *85.   Evelina. }
    *86.   Daniel (II).
    *87.   Delilah.
    *88.   Margaretta.
    *89.   Mary.

29. William Ficklen, son of Benjamin (I), married Paulina Hill, of Stafford county. Both he and his wife died at an early age. (An account of sales of William Ficklen, of record in Stafford, and dated 5 December, 1826, would indicate that he died in that year.) They left two sons and one daughter:‡

    90.   William, married Jane Dickerson of Stafford Springs, Va., and, in 1839, emigrated to Randolph county, Mo., where he spent the remainder of his life. He died 5 December, 1874, and is buried in the Old Eldad burying ground, near where he lived. To this couple were born eleven children:§   (a) Lewis Wil-

†Data concerning Daniel Ficklen and descendants has been taken from the old Bible and from a booklet entitled "Excerpta from the Genealogies of the Dorsey, Anderson, Ficklen, and Miller Families," compiled by Achsah Van Dyke Miller-Taylor, of Louisville, Ky., and Florence Griffith-Miller, of Asheville, N. C., and also from letters written by Mrs. Leila M. Ficklen, of Memphis, and Wm. T. Ficklen, of Paris, Ky.

‡Data concerning William Ficklen and family was taken, except where otherwise indicated, from Slaughter MS., and Slaughter W. Ficklin's pamphlet of 1870.

§Information concerning the Ficklins of Randolph county, Missouri, was given by Lewis W. Ficklin, of Moberly, Missouri.

liam, who married Mary Ann Baker and died in August, 1860. They had one child, Lewis William, Jr., who is a merchant in Moberly, Mo. (b) Horace Buckner, who married Margaret Baker and died 10 March, 1906. They reared a family of nine children, all of whom reside in Randolph county. (c) Paulina, (d) Delia, deceased; (e) Susan M., (f) Mary L., who never married; (g) Leonard M., deceased; (h) Catherine Jane, who married Minor Clifton of Randolph county; (i) Henry Clay, who married Adeline Rothwell and lives in Marceline, Mo.; (j) James Richards, who married (1) Belle McCully, (2) Annie Barnes; (k) George W., who married (1) Alice Henderson, (2) Bettie Pierce.

91. Paulina, married a Mr. Norman, had several children. One daughter, Susan, married A. D. Smith, and lived in Fauquier county, Virginia, and had several children.

92. Leonard, married Teresa Hill of Culpeper county, 1844.

30. Benjamin Ficklin (II), son of Benjamin (I). The following is taken from Rev. Edgar Wood's "History of Albemarle County, Virginia" (1901):

"Benjamin Ficklin became a citizen of Albemarle about 1814, and is described in one place as being from Frederick County and in another from Culpeper. Either then or shortly afterwards he entered the Baptist Ministry. He purchased in the western part of the county upwards of thirteen hundred acres, and his residence for twenty years, called Pleasant Green, was the place adjoining Crozet on the west, now occupied by Abraham Wayland. He was appointed to a seat on the county bench in 1819. In 1822 he proposed to sell his lands with a design of removing to Ohio or Indiana. This purpose, however, was abandoned, and in 1832 he removed to Charlottesville, where for a number of years he engaged in the manufacture of tobacco. He was noted for his uprightness and decision of character.

"At the time of his removal to Charlottesville, the state of things in the town, morally and religiously was far from being unexceptionable.

In a clandestine manner most of the stores did more business on Sunday than other days. Negroes came in large numbers for the purposes of traffic. Great quantities of liquor were sold. In the later hours of that day, the roads leading from town were lined with men and women in all stages of drunkenness, some staggering with difficulty, others lying helplessly by the wayside.

"Mr. Ficklin set himself vigorously to remedy these evils. He warned the merchants that every violation of the Sunday law would be visited with the highest penalty. A similar warning was given to the negroes; and by the lively application of the lash to those who neglected it, the towns and roads were soon cleaned of transgressors. Sabbath observance put on a new face. The comfort of worshippers, and the general order of the community were vastly promoted. So impartial was the old man in the execution of his duty, that when one of his own wagons, sent out to sell tobacco, trespassed on the sacred hours in reaching home, he imposed a fine upon himself. It is said that a member of the bar remonstrated with him on what he considered his excessive zeal, and stated by way of illustration that in the preparation of his cases, he had often been obliged to work on Sundays, whereupon Mr. Ficklin at once fined him on his own confession. Altogether the whole county was laid under many obligations to his courage, efficiency, and public spirit.

"His last years were over-clouded with business reverses. He closed his earthly career during the war, in the last days of 1864."

He married, first, Miss Lucy Jones, and had one son:

    *93. William Samuel.

He married, second, 1816, Miss Ellen Slaughter, daughter of Captain William Slaughter of Culpeper county, Virginia, and had six children:†

    *94. Slaughter W.
    *95. Lucy A.
    *96. M. Elizabeth.
    *97. Ellen M.
    *98. Benjamin F.
    *99. Susan M.

---

†The account of the family and descendants of Benjamin (II) Ficklin, son of Benjamin, was taken from Slaughter W. Ficklin's pamphlet of 1870, and from letters written by his sister, Mrs. S. M. Hardesty, who resides in Washington, D. C.

Benjamin Ficklin (II) of Albemarle County, Virginia, and Wife, Ellen (Slaughter) Ficklin. (From photographs taken in 1856.)

31. Mary Ficklin, daughter of Benjamin (I), married a Mr. White, emigrated to Fleming county, Kentucky, and had one child:†
    *100.. Mary White.
32. Susan Ficklin, daughter of Benjamin (I), married Rev. Edward Matthews, and lived in Baltimore. She died childless in 1851.†
33. Elizabeth Ficklin, daughter of Benjamin (I), married Dr. Elbert, and moved to Logan county, Ohio. They had two daughters and one son:†
    *101. Fanny Elbert.
    *102. Elizabeth Elbert.
    *103. John Downes Elbert.
34. Sarah Ficklin, daughter of Benjamin (I), married F. Bell. They emigrated to Ohio, and had two children:†
    *104. Fielding Bell.
    *105. Mary Bell.

35. John Herndon Ficklin, son of Thomas and grandson of William (II), is first mentioned in a deed recorded in Spottsylvania county, Virginia, 1772. He was a private in Capt. Jacob Stucker's company, Col. Richard Johnson's regiment of Kentucky mounted infantry at the Battle of the Thames (Filson Club publication, "Battle of the Thames"). He was a Baptist minister (Slaughter MS.) and missionary to the Indians of the South and Southwest. He founded the Choctaw Academy in Scott county, Kentucky, which is believed to have been the first school for Indian boys in America. In this he had the hearty co-operation of Col. Richard M. Johnson, his old commander and afterwards vice-president of the United States. It was his ambition to make this the national educational center for Redmen, but with the death of both Ficklin and Johnson the school died for lack of leadership. The burning of the older records of Scott county has made it difficult to learn much concerning this John Ficklin or his family. His wife was Anna Herndon and to them were born two sons:‡

†Data concerning Mary, Susan, Elizabeth, and Sarah Ficklin, daughters of the elder Benjamin, was taken from Slaughter W. Ficklin's pamphlet of 1870.
‡Excepting where otherwise indicated, data concerning John Herndon Ficklin and descendants was gleaned from letters written by Mrs. Frances True, of Espanola, New Mexico, and Nat C. Ficklin, of Brown Station, Mo.

106. Asa, who emigrated to Callaway county, Mo., in 1818, and married a Jenkins. He was a slave owner and died about the close of the Civil War. He had a son, Thomas A., who was a veteran of the War with Mexico and also Civil War (Confederate), and married America Ann Craig, died 1897, daughter of Nat Craig. Thomas A., died in Columbia, Mo., 6 May, 1907. He had twelve children, of whom five are living: Mrs. Sarah Fields, of Mexico, Mo.; Nat C. Ficklin, of Brown Station, Mo.; A. W. Ficklin, of Fayetteville, Ark.; L. W. Ficklin, of Bowie, Tex.; and Mrs. M. G. Headrick, of Grear county, Okla.

107. Benjamin, who emigrated to Missouri with his brother and died shortly after the Civil War. He married Amanda Russell Abbott. Mrs. Ann Kennet, of Millersburg, Mo., is thought to be a daughter of this couple.

36. Joseph Ficklin, son of Thomas and grandson of William (II), was appointed consul at St. Bartholomew Island, 26 April, 1816, and served there till 1820 (Records State Dept.). Was appointed postmaster at Lexington, 11 January, 1822, by President Monroe, at which time he was editor of the Kentucky Gazette. He served continuously till July, 1841, and was re-appointed by President Tyler, 29 March, 1843, and served till 4 October, 1850. His administration was noted for its efficiency. The mail was carried in four-horse post coaches. It was during the latter part of his administration that the adhesive postage stamp came into use. These were printed on sheets and had to be cut apart with scissors. He is remembered by some of the older citizens, as a very large man who was always followed by a small dog. He owned considerable property about the city which, at his death (he having no children nor relatives), was left to his colored servants. (Data taken from Thos. L. Walker's Hist. of Lexington Postoffice.)

Joseph Ficklin was a trustee of Transylvania University and was instrumental in the up-building of that institution ("Transylvania University"—Filson Club publication). This Joseph Ficklin was postmaster

Joseph Ficklin, of Lexington, Kentucky.
(From Thos. L. Walker's History of the Lexington Postoffice.)

at Russellville, Kentucky, from 1 October, 1802, to 25 December, 1812 (records of Russellville postoffice, and also Collins' History of Kentucky, vol. 1, p. 487). He and his wife, Polly L. (*nee* Campbell), disposed of the last of their property in Russellville in 1826 (Logan county records).

A marriage contract between Joseph Ficklin and Polly L. Campbell is on record at Lexington, and likewise the will of the latter (Polly L. Ficklin), dated 1849. In this instrument she mentions her husband as then living and emancipates her slaves and devises her property to them very much as her husband did his two or three years later. Thomas L. Walker, mentioned above, writes that Joseph Harrison, one of the oldest citizens of Lexington, remembers well Joseph Ficklin and wife, Polly L.

37. William Augustus Ficklin, son of Thomas and grandson of William (II), was a native of Virginia, but moved to Kentucky and afterwards to Washington county, Missouri. He married Elizabeth Kenner Williams, likewise a native of Virginia, and is known to have had three children:†

  *108.   Orlando Bell.
  109.   Augustus Williams, of whom nothing known.
  110.   Mary Catherine, of whom nothing known.

---

40. Jared (or Jarrett) Ficklin, son of John and grandson of William (II), was probably born about 1782, in Spottsylvania county, Virginia. The first record of him is in the census returns for Jessamine county, Ky., 1810, in which he is mentioned as the head of a family, "Jarrott Ficklin, free white males, 26 to 45, one; free white males under 10, one; free white females, 16 to 26, one; slaves, 3." The next record which mentions him is an entry in the register of Mt. Pleasant Baptist church, "Jarrot Ficklin's colored woman, 'Milly,' joined Mt. Pleasant Baptist church, May, 1811." He must have been living in Jessamine when his father died, 6 June, 1819, for he is named an executor in the will. He moved shortly afterwards to

---

†Data concerning William Augustus Ficklin was taken from Chapman Bros. Hist. of Coles County, Ill., Chicago, 1885. The list of children, excepting Orlando, was taken from letter written by Mrs. Emma W. Ficklin, of Kerman, Cal., daughter-in-law of Orlando B. Ficklin. She has a copy of an old book which once belonged to Orlando's father and bears the inscription, "William Augustus Ficklin, M.D."

Mercer county, now Boyle. His wife was Elizabeth Bowman Dunklin,†
who was born in Laurens county, S. C., 6 January, 1789, and died in
Boyle county, Ky., 22 May, 1839. They lived on a large farm which
Elizabeth Ficklin had inherited from her uncle, John Bowman. This
farm is bounded by a bend in the Dix river near where the Cincinnati and
Southern railroad crosses that stream. They are both buried in Danville,
Ky. Their children were:

    *111.   Joseph, Sr.

    *112.   John.

    *113.   Robert.

    *114.   William.

    *115.   Sarah Ann.

Elizabeth Ficklin survived her husband, who died about 1835, and
married a Mr. Long, and had two children, who, after her death, went to
Texas.

42.   John Ficklin, son of John and grandson of William (II), was a corporal
in Capt. James C. Price's Company, Col. Lewis' regiment of Kentucky
Volunteers, War of 1812-14 (Young's History of Jessamine County).
He married Judith Goodloe, and settled in Montgomery county, Kentucky, in a neighborhood known as Antioch. They had seven children:‡

---

†The first record of a Dunklin of this branch is of Joseph Dunklin, of Laurens county, S. C.,
whose wife was Jane Caroline Worthen. Two of their children were Joseph, whose son, Daniel, was
once governor of Missouri, and John, who married Mary Bowman, daughter of Jacob Bowman and wife,
Sarah, at Tumbling Shoals, on Reedy river, in 1788. Jacob Bowman was assassinated by Tories in 1780.
John Dunklin was captain of South Carolina militia during the Revolution, and after that war, emigrated
with his family to Virginia. About 1800 he moved to Kentucky, and in 1820 to New Madrid county,
Mo., where he died. He and his wife are buried on their old plantation in that county and the inscrip-
tions on their grave stones are as follows:
"John Dunklin, died August 13, 1834, aged 69 years."
"Mary Dunklin, wife of John Dunklin, died April 13, 1836, aged 68 years."
Their children were Elizabeth Bowman, married Jared Ficklin; Sarah Stevens, born 7 November,
1790, and lived to the age of 98, married Pendleton Thomas, two of her children, Mrs. Joanna P. Proctor,
of Santa Rosa, Calif., and Mrs. E. P. Burnsides, of Bryantsville, Ky., are still living (1911) at advanced
ages; Harriet Shipp, born 26 December, 1792, married Hardin Perkins, and has son, Ben H. Perkins,
living at Middlesboro, Ky.; William, has grandson, W. E. Sherwood, living at St. Joseph, Mo.; John,
born 4 July, 1797; Joseph, born 2 December, 1799; James, born 4 February, 1803; Nancy, born 12
March, 1806, married David Imboden; Jefferson and Madison, twins, born 8 January, 1809—Mrs. Nannie
Brownell, of West Plains, Mo., is a daughter of Jefferson.
Mr. Wm. E. Sherwood, of St. Joseph, Mo., mentioned above, is preparing a history of the Dunklin
and Bowman families.

‡The account of this John Ficklin and family was given by Henry Scott, Sr., of Owingsville, Ky.,
and Thomas Ficklin, of Stanberry, Mo.

116. Charlotte.
117. Catherine.
118. Margaret.
119. John.
120. George.
121. Clifton.
122. Benjamin.

[Of the above, Charlotte married Wm. Miller, and Catherine married Milton P. Stevens. Most of this family moved to Illinois and nothing further has been learned concerning them.]

43. William Ficklin, son of John and grandson of William (II), lived at Mt. Sterling, Ky. He was born in Virginia. His wife was Frances Walker. They had a son (probably other children also):

*123. Jarrett.†

44. Thomas Ficklin, son of John and grandson of William (II), was a private in Capt. Mason Singleton's company of Jessamine county, Kentucky, Volunteers, War of 1812-14 (Young's History of Jessamine County). He was married twice, but had no children by his first wife. He married, second, Mary Goodloe, sister of Judith Goodloe (see No. 42), and about ninety years ago settled in what was known as the Peal Oak neighborhood in Bath county, Kentucky, about seven miles from Owingsville. He operated a tannery and died about 1864. Their children were:‡

*124. Ellen.
*125. John.
*126. James Price.
*127. Newton.
*128. Joseph.
*129. Thomas.
*130. Madison.

---

†The account of this William Ficklin and descendants was given by his grandson, A. Walker Ficklin, of Jeffersonville, Ky.

‡The account of this Thomas Ficklin and descendants was given by his grandson, Thomas Ficklin, of Stanberry, Mo.

46.   Charles Ficklin, son of John and grandson of William (II), lived at Danville, Ky., for a few years, but moved from there to Texas, about seventy years ago, and all trace of him has been lost.

---

52.   Margaret Ficklin, daughter of Joseph and granddaughter of William (II), was probably born in Spottsylvania county, Virginia. The following dates were taken from the family Bible of her daughter (Sarah Ann Edmunds), which is now in the possession of Mrs. Catherine Read, of Decatur, Texas: Margaret Ficklin was born 19 March, 1782. Joseph Pulliam was born 8 February, 1771. Margaret Ficklin and Joseph Pulliam were married 5 August, 1800. Margaret Pulliam died 1 January, 1849. Joseph Pulliam died 27 October, 1854.

Both are buried on the old Ficklin farm at Scottville, Ky. Joseph Pulliam was a son of Benjamin Pulliam. They had twelve children. The dates of birth of the first five of these are recorded on a sampler worked by Margaret Pulliam. This sampler is now in the possession of Miss Louise Edmunds, of Willard, N. M.

131.   Nancy, born 1801, married Robert Bradley, of Hopkinsville, Ky., and had two children, Robert, and Louisa Richards.

132.   Martha, born 1803, married Thomas McFarland, of Hopkinsville, Ky., and reared six children.

133.   Robert Ficklin, born 1805, married Eveline Ellis and had nine children, one of whom, Robert Ficklin Pulliam (II), is living on the old farm at Scottville.

134.   Elizabeth, born 1807, married William Hopson, of Hopkinsville, Ky., and had seven children.

135.   Sarah Newby, born 1809, married Richard W. Edmunds, of Amherst county, Virginia, and had six children. Miss Louise Edmunds, of Willard, N. M., is a granddaughter of theirs.

136.   Joseph, never married.

137. Augustus S., married (1) Rebecca Martin and had seven children; and (2) Adeline Priddy and had six children. His first child, Margaret, married John J. Woolery and resides at Garden City, Mo., and has a daughter, Leonora, who married T. F. Flaherty and lives in Kansas City, Mo.

138. Benjamin, never married.

139. Catherine, married (1) Al. Wickware and had three children; and (2) Phillips and had two children.

140. Lucinda, married Joseph Venable and had five children.

141. James, married Sarah Pulliam, his cousin, and had five children.

142. Margaret, died in infancy.

---

53. Henry Kenyon Ficklin, son of John and grandson of Thomas (I), was born 12 February, 1792; died 8 August, 1810.

54. Joseph Kenyon Ficklin, son of John and grandson of Thomas (I), was born 6 March, 1793. Operated a ferry on the Ohio river at Maysville in 1818. Lived at Mt. Carmel, Ill. Married, but died without issue.

55. John Minton Ficklin, son of John and grandson of Thomas (I), was born 23 September, 1794. Lived in St. Louis. Died 15 April, 1832.

56. Lucy Ficklin, daughter of John and granddaughter of Thomas (I), was born in Fauquier county, Virginia, 19 October, 1795; died 3 March, 1837. She married Charles Killgore, son of Samuel and Mary Killgore, of Cumberland county, Pennsylvania, born 17 May, 1777; died 8 December, 1858. He was a farmer, and one of the foremost citizens of Mason county, Kentucky, where they lived. Their children were:

*143. Anthony Killgore.
*144. Julia Ann Killgore.
*145. John Ficklin Killgore.
*146. Robert James Killgore.
*147. Joseph Henry Killgore.
*148. Lucy Killgore.

*149.   Angelina Killgore.
*150.   Melvina Killgore.
*151.   Charles Henry Killgore.
*152.   Sarah Ann Killgore.
*153.   Judith Ellen Killgore.

57.   Thomas Ficklin, son of John and grandson of Thomas (I), was born 29 July, 1797.   Died without issue 11 August, 1830.

58.   Judith Kenyon Ficklin, daughter of John and granddaughter of Thomas (I), was born 16 February, 1799.   Died 30 October, 1828.

59.   James Kenyon Ficklin, son of John and grandson of Thomas (I), was born 30 August, 1800.   Lived in Cincinnati.   Died without issue in September, 1847.

60.   Robert Ficklin, son of John and grandson of Thomas (I), was born 5 August, 1802; died 6 February, 1887.   He lived at Maysville, Kentucky, where he engaged in the dry goods business.   His wife was Alice Ann Cox, born 15 November, 1821; died 10 July, 1852, daughter of George and Anne Cox, of that city.   Their children were:
*154.   Anna Hopkinson.
*155.   Caroline Kenyon.
*156.   Allen Bruce.
*157.   Alice.
*158.   Lucy Adelaide.
*159.   Robert.
*160.   Horatio.

69.   Famous Ficklin, son of Benjamin, grandson of Anthony, lived in Richmond county, Virginia.   He married Elizabeth, daughter of Christopher DeAtley.   (See will of Christopher DeAtley, of record in Richmond county, dated 27 September, 1793.)   He had children as follows:
*161.   Christopher DeAtley.
162.   John D., whose will was probated in Richmond county, 2 August, 1841.
163.   Leroy D., whose will was probated in Richmond county, 6 January, 1834.

164.   Ann, who died in Richmond county.   Will probated 7
February, 1825.

164½.Sarah, who died in Richmond county.   Will probated
4 October, 1830.

72.   James Grant Ficklen, son of Fielding (I) and Elizabeth (Fant) Ficklen,
was born in 1794, at the old homestead in Culpeper county, Virginia.   He
was a man of great energy and ability, being first engaged in farming, but
later as a merchant.   He lived at "Belleville," a handsome estate near
Winchester, Virginia.   He married Miss Katherine Davenport, of Jefferson county, Virginia.   He had a high appreciation of the value of education, and early employed the best classical teachers to instruct his children.
Failing health compelled him to move to Winchester, where, in 1842, he
died at the early age of fifty-two.   He is buried in Mount Hebron cemetery in that city.   Six children survived him:†

*165.   John Fielding.
*166.   Ellen Douglas.
*167.   James Burwell.
*168.   Nannie.
*169.   Susan Matthews.
*170.   Rebecca Davenport.

73.   George Ficklen son of Fielding (I) and Elizabeth (Fant) Ficklen, married, first, Miss Fannie Kennon, of Kentucky, and resided in Culpeper
county, Virginia.   He married, second, Miss Eviline Spindle, of Culpeper county; and third, Jane Johnston Dunlop (nee Bankhead), of Caroline county, 6 October, 1848 (Caroline county records, also Hayden's
"Virginia Genealogies").   His children, as follows, resulted from the
first marriage:‡

*171.   Elizabeth.
*172.   Harriet.
*173.   Fannie M.

†Data concerning James Grant Ficklen and descendants was furnished by Mrs. E. J. Harrison, of Kingston, N. Y., Mrs. Kate Ficklen Marshall, of Lynchburg, Va., and Mrs. Daviette Carbell Ficklen, of Washington, D. C.

‡Data concerning George Ficklen and Joseph Burwell Ficklen and their descendants was furnished by Harry C. Ficklen, of Danville, Va.

*174. Mary Virginia.
*175. Laura.
*176. Joseph E.
*177. Sarah.
*178. Louisa.
*179. Georgia.
*180. Lucy.

74. Joseph Burwell Ficklen, son of Fielding (I) and Elizabeth (Fant) Ficklen, was born in 1800, lived first at "Belmont," near Falmouth, Virginia, but moved later to Fredericksburg. He married, first, Ellen McGehee, of Milton, North Carolina, who died without issue. He married, second, in 1847, Anne Eliza Fitzhugh, of Fredericksburg. He died about 1870, and is buried at Fredericksburg. His second wife died 10 August, 1907, aged over ninety years. Their children were:

*181. Joseph Burwell, Jr.
*182. Edmonia Fitzhugh.
*183. Nannie.
*184. William Fitzhugh.
*185. George.
*186. John Rose.

75. Fielding Ficklen (II), son of Fielding (I) and Elizabeth (Fant) Ficklen, married Miss Frances Wingfield, was very prominent as a physician and lived in Washington, Georgia, to which he emigrated in 1824, and where he is buried. Their children were:†

*187. James.
*188. Samuel.
*189. Joseph Burwell.
*190. Elizabeth.
*191. Georgia.
*192. Sarah.
*193. Mary.
*194. William.

---

†Data concerning Dr. Fielding Ficklen and descendants was furnished by Mrs. Boyce Ficklen, of Washington, Georgia.
    Something of the war time experience of this family may be found in Miss Fannie Andrews' "War Time Journal of a Georgia Girl."—D. Appleton & Co.

*195.   John.
*196.   Ella.
*197.   Boyce.

6.   Sarah Ficklen, daughter of Fielding (I) and Elizabeth (Fant) Ficklen, was born 27 August, 1797.   She married William Brown, 1816, and lived at Locust Hill on Thornton river in Culpeper county, Virginia. She died at Glenwood, in Rappahannock county, 1 December, 1875. Their children were:†

*198.   Ann Brown.
*199.   Lucinda Brown.
*200.   Henrietta Brown.
*201.   James F. Brown.
*202.   Charles Gideon Brown.
*203.   Sarah William Brown.

7.   Harriet Ficklen, daughter of Fielding (I) and Elizabeth (Fant) Ficklen, was born in Culpeper county, Virginia, 9 August, 1796, and 24 December, 1813, married William Slaughter of that county.   This couple lived at the "Hermitage" (near the Madison county line) till 1847. The remainder of their lives was spent at Fredericksburg, where they are buried.   Harriet Ficklen Slaughter died 28 August, 1881.   Their children were:‡

*204.   Elizabeth Susan Slaughter.
*205.   Franklin Slaughter.
*206.   Montgomery Slaughter.
*207.   J. Warren Slaughter.
*208.   Albert Slaughter.
*209.   Sarah Anne Slaughter.
*210.   Harriet Jane Slaughter.
*211.   Eliza Frances Slaughter.
*212.   Matilda Slaughter.
*213.   Joseph Fant Slaughter.
*214.   Joseph Fielding Slaughter.

---

†Data concerning Sarah Ficklen and descendants was furnished by Judge W. W. Moffett, of alem, Va.
‡Data concerning Harriet Ficklen and descendants was furnished by Harry C. Ficklen, of Danille, Va.

78. Eliza Ficklen, daughter of Fielding (I) and Elizabeth (Fant) Ficklen, married Dr. Mark Reid, 1820, of Rappahannock county, Virginia. She died 1841. They lived at Woodville, in that county, and had several children:†

    *215. Henrietta Reid.
    *216. William B. Reid.
    *217. Virginia Pocahontas Reid.
    *218. Sarah Reid.
    *219. Eliza Reid.
    *220. Nannie B. Reid.
    *221. Matilda Baker Reid.

79. Noble V. Ficklen, son of Daniel (I) and Delilah (Leonard) Ficklen, was born 5 March, 1795, and died 15 August, 1835. He married 21 April, 1825, Charlotte Pearce, who died 10 October, 1829. They lived in Flemingsburg, Ky. Their children were:

    222. Wm. Pickett, born 24 May, 1826; died in Flemingsburg, Ky., 25 October, 1862. He never married.
    223. Lucinda C., born 4 July, 1828. She also is dead.

80. William Ficklen, son of Daniel (I) and Delilah (Leonard) Ficklen, was born in Stafford county, Virginia, 25 October, 1797, and married Elizabeth Threlkill 3 May, 1821, and lived at Elizaville, Kentucky. Elizabeth Ficklen died 7 June, 1838. William married, second, Clarissa Corwine, 25 November, 1838. He was a noted stock raiser and trader. Removing to Mason county, he laid out the village of Fairview. Later he engaged in the wholesale coffee trade at Maysville. He died 1 September, 1864, and is buried in Paris, Kentucky. To William and his first wife were born:

    224. Ary, who married Alexander D. Bishop; died leaving several children.
    225. Elizabeth, married W. H. Cassidy, and lived at Newport, Ky. Their children were: Charles, Robert, George, James, Elizabeth, Frank, William.

---

†Data concerning Eliza Ficklen and descendants was furnished by Judge W. W. Moffett, of Salem, Va.

William Threlkill Ficklen, of Paris, Kentucky, born 16 September, 1827—thought to be the senior member of the Ficklin family in America, 1912.

226. Daniel, married a Miss Hunter. He had one son and a daughter, and died in early life.
227. William Threlkill, born in Elizaville, Kentucky, 16 September, 1827. He is a bachelor, hale and hearty at the age of 85, and lives at Paris, Kentucky.
228. Paulina, married her brother-in-law, A. D. Bishop. She has no children, and is living in Covington, Kentucky.
229. Mary, married F. M. Chase, and lives in Covington, Kentucky.

81. Malinda Ficklen, daughter of Daniel (I) and Delilah (Leonard) Ficklen, was born 10 March, 1800. Married John H. Botts 4 January, 1820. Their children were:
230. Daniel Ficklen Botts, died 6 December, 1832.
231. Benjamin Botts, married Juliet E. Dorsey, and had several children. He was sheriff of Fleming county, Kentucky, for several years.
232. Alexander Botts—nothing has been learned concerning him.
233. Amelia Botts, died 21 November, 1832.
234. Mary Botts, married Dr. Allen, and had several children.
235. Malinda Botts, married in 1866, and lived in Fleming county, Kentucky.

82. Sarah Ficklen, daughter of Daniel (I) and Delilah (Leonard) Ficklen, was born 7 April, 1802. Married James Stuart 23 March, 1826. They lived in Paris, Kentucky, and had eight children:
236. Mary Jane Stuart, married Dr. Fleming, and had several children.
237. Delilah Stuart.
238. Elizabeth Stuart.
239. Caroline Stuart.
240. William Stuart, married and lived in St. Louis.
241. John Stuart, married Miss Georgia Williams, and resided at Paris, Kentucky.
242. James Stuart.
243. Daniel Stuart.

83.   James L. Ficklen, son of Daniel (I) and Delilah (Leonard) Ficklen, was born 9 March, 1809, married Mary M. Swindler, of Kanawha, W. Va., 5 March, 1829. They had no children, and lived at Owensboro, Kentucky. He died in 1888. His widow died in 1894.

84.   Caroline Ficklen, daughter of Daniel (I) and Delilah (Leonard) Ficklen, was born 19 December, 1807. Married John Stuart 14 December, 1837. They had three children:
>   244.   Daniel Stuart.
>   245.   Delilah Stuart.
>   246.   Jane Stuart, married Dr. Abney. They had no children.

85.   Evalina Ficklen, twin of Caroline (No. 84), married James Wrenche 25 November, 1832. They had two sons:
>   247.   James Wrenche, married and lived in New York.
>   248.   Noble Wrenche, was in the Confederate service and after the war went to North Carolina, and married there.

[Evalina Wrenche afterwards married a Mr. Allen.]

86.   Daniel Ficklen (II), son of Daniel (I) and Delilah (Leonard) Ficklen, was born 13 April, 1810. Married Achsah Van Dyke Anderson, Thursday, 5 February, 1835. Achsah Anderson was born 24 August, 1815. They lived at Elizaville, Kentucky. He died in 1847, leaving four children:
>   *249.   Lucy Pickett.
>   *250.   Charles Leonard.
>   *251.   Amelia S.
>   *252.   Elizabeth.

[Achsah Ficklen survived her husband, and afterwards married Arthur Berry. Two children were born: Austin Berry, born 15 June, 1852, who is living in Owensboro, Kentucky, and Mary Ellen Berry, born 14 January, 1859.]

87.   Delilah Ficklen, daughter of Daniel (I) and Delilah (Leonard) Ficklen, was born 2 October, 1812. She married Dillard Hazelrigg 29 October, 1843. They had one child, a daughter, and resided at Mt. Sterling, Kentucky.

Slaughter W. Ficklin, of Charlottesville, Virginia.

88. Margaretta Ficklen, daughter of Daniel (I) and Delilah (Leonard) Ficklen, was born 17 July, 1815. Married Andrew Howe 19 September, 1839, and lived at Poplar Plains, Kentucky. They had two children:

    253. Robert Howe.

    254. Mary Howe, married Dr. Yantes. They had several children and lived at Poplar Plains, Kentucky.

89. Mary Ficklen, daughter of Daniel (I) and Delilah (Leonard) Ficklen, was born 25 March, 1818. Married George Summers 12 September, 1840. They had ten children, but nothing is known of them.

---

93. William Samuel Ficklin, son of Banjamin (II) and Lucy (Jones) Ficklin, married Miss Harper, of Georgia. Had four children, three daughters and one son—all married and died at an early age. He lived in Iowa.

94. Slaughter W. Ficklin son of Benjamin (II) and second wife, Ellen (Slaughter) Ficklin, published in 1870 a history of the Ficklin family since 1720, the first and only printed account of the family in America up to that time (see Preface). He was a captain in the Confederate Army. He married Miss Caroline Wilkins, of Baltimore and lived at "Belmont," near Charlottesville, Virginia. He died in 1886. They had two sons:

    255. William Joseph, who lived at Belmont till his death in February, 1906.

    256. John Slaughter, who died in 1862, aged seven years.

95. Lucy A. Ficklin, daughter of Benjamin (II) and second wife, Ellen (Slaughter) Ficklin, married F. D. Brockman. She died in early life leaving one child, an infant, who died a few months later.

96. M. Elizabeth Ficklin, daughter of Benjamin (II) and second wife, Ellen (Slaughter) Ficklin, married Elijah Dunkum. They had two daughters:

    257. Nellie Dunkum, who married Henry King of Alabama, and had two children.

    258. Lucy Dunkum.

97. Ellen M. Ficklin, daughter of Benjamin (II) and second wife, Ellen (Slaughter) Ficklin, married Dr. Brown. They had no children.

98. Benjamin F. Ficklin, son of Benjamin (II) and second wife, Ellen (Slaughter) Ficklin, was the most picturesque and widest known of the Ficklins in America. He emigrated to the Far West before the Civil War, and superintended the Overland Stage Line and Pony Express from Independence, Missouri, to the Pacific ocean. (An interesting account of this enterprise may be found in Root and Connelly's "Overland Stage to California." Topeka, Kansas, 1901.)

At the outbreak of the Civil War, he went to his native state, and he became quartermaster for Stonewall Jackson's famous army corps. Later he operated a blockade runner and made many trips between European ports, Nassau and Charleston, S. C., conveying supplies and munitions of war to the Confederacy.

The following is taken from the London Standard, in which an article appeared by the Hon. F. Lawley, 1895 (exact date of issue unknown) :†

"Ben Ficklin was a Virginian by birth, and during the Civil War was generally employed by the Confederate Government in controlling the Red Indians on the other side of the Mississippi River, and the lawless whites, who had lived so long with the Comanches and Apaches, that they had caught the manners, habits and ideas of Cochise, Magnus, Colorado, and other great sachems or chiefs of the redskin tribes. On many occasions, however, Ben Ficklin passed weeks at a time in Richmond, Virginia, and I never lost an opportunity of listening to the conversation of one of the best and most interesting talkers I have ever met.

"In appearance he somewhat resembled the late Sir Richard Burton, and gave you the impression that no moment, either by day or night, would have found him unprepared to go into action right away against any foe that he could be called upon to meet.

"He was a man of forty-five or more when I first met him, and, before the war, had been connected all over the voiceless solitudes of the Far West with running stage coaches and pony expresses through districts

† Cuttings loaned by P. Berney Ficklin, of Tasburgh, England.

Benjamin F. Ficklin, Noted Plainsman.

swarming with redmen, where nature herself is often more formidable than the wiliest Comanche who ever took a scalp. Certainly his experiences, including hair-breadth escapes without number, were more exciting than Fenimore Cooper's 'Last of the Mohicans' or Dick Bird's 'Nick of the Woods,' and after listening to him for a couple of hours, you could not help being ashamed of yourself for having only the tame and prosaic life of civilization, which has in it nothing of the peril and 'snap' and still less of the camaraderie of frontier warfare   *   *   *''

Ben Ficklin never married. He died in 1871 at the Willard Hotel in Washington, D. C., having choked to death on a fish bone.

99. Susan M. Ficklin, daughter of Benjamin (II) and second wife, Ellen (Slaughter) Ficklin, married Dr. J. R. L. Hardesty of Rockingham county, Virginia, 18 June, 1856. They lived for a few years in Wheeling, West Virginia, but later moved to Washington, D. C., where they still reside. They celebrated their 50th wedding anniversary 18 June, 1906. They had ten children, of whom five are living:

> 259. Isaac Lee Hardesty, lives in Pittsburg. Has been in the office of the Pennsylvania Railroad over twenty years. He is married and has no children.
>
> 260. Roberta Hardesty, married Capt. McBlain, U. S. A., who died in Houston, Texas, and was interred in the National Cemetery at Arlington. They resided at Ft. Riley, Kansas, and after his death she was appointed postmistress at that place by President Roosevelt and has served two terms. They had one son, John F. McBlain, who is now a lad of eleven years.
>
> 261. Ben Ficklin Hardesty lives in Chicago and is in railroad work also. He is married and has two children: Elizabeth Harris and Josephine Roberta.
>
> 262. Fred S. Hardesty, lives in Washington, D. C. Married Eustacia Boyle. They have two children: Eustacia B. and Fred Lee.

263. William Slaughter Hardesty is a physician living in Washington, D. C. He is a graduate of George Washington University and holds a position with the United States Geological Survey and Interstate Commerce Commission. He married Miss Stuart and has no children.

---

100. Mary White, daughter of ———— White and Mary (Ficklin) White (No. 31), married Nelson Fant. They had two daughters and one son:

264. Louisa White, married Festus Williams of Missouri, and had two children.

265. Juliet White, married and died in early life.

266. William Slaughter White, married Miss Saunders and resided at Sherbourne, Kentucky. They had several children.

---

101. Fanny Elbert, daughter of Dr. Elbert and Elizabeth (Ficklin) Elbert, married a Mr. Everett, who died after a few years, leaving her with two children. They lived in Ohio.

102. Elizabeth Elbert, daughter of Dr. Elbert and Elizabeth (Ficklin) Elbert, married Rev. Mr. Walker of the Methodist church. They lived in Ohio and had no children.

103. John Downes Elbert, son of Dr. Elbert and Elizabeth (Ficklin) Elbert, married Miss Hilt of Indiana. They emigrated to Van Buren county, Iowa, at an early period of its settlement. He died in the summer of 1855, leaving a widow and several children: Anna, Samuel H., Rebecca, Leroy, Benjamin and Daniel. Samuel H. Elbert, mentioned above, married in 1865, a daughter of Governor Evans of Colorado, and was afterwards territorial governor of Colorado, and one of the first justices of its Supreme Court. Elbert county, Colorado, was named for him.

Anna Elbert married Judge Townsend, and resided at Albia, Iowa. They had several children.

Rebecca Elbert, married a Mr. Clark, and resided also at Albia, Iowa. They had several children.

Leroy Elbert was a graduate of West Point. Never married. Was a captain in the Federal Army and died during the Civil War.

---

104. Fielding Bell, son of F. Bell and Sarah (Ficklin) Bell (No. 34), married and emigrated to Missouri. Nothing more is known of him.

105. Mary Bell, daughter of F. Bell and Sarah (Ficklin) Bell (No. 34), married a Mr. Caruthers, and resided a long while in Wheeling, West Virginia. She survived her husband and moved to Bloomfield. They had three children, one a daughter, Charlotte Caruthers, married a Mr. Trimble, a lawyer, who ranked as colonel, and was killed during the Civil War.

---

108. Orlando B. Ficklin, son of William Augustus, was one of the foremost citizens of Illinois, a broad-minded statesman, and more widely known in public life than any other member of the Ficklin family. The following biography is taken from Chapman Bros.' History of Coles County, Ill., Chicago, 1885:

"Orlando B. Ficklin, one of the most prominent and useful citizens who ever honored Coles county, and one who in many respects did more in its behalf than any other man, was born December 16, 1808.

"He was the son of William and Elizabeth Kenner (Williams) Ficklin, natives of Virginia, but who removed to Kentucky where their son, Orlando, was born. He received a practical education in the schools of Kentucky and Missouri, whither his parents subsequently removed, and passed one year in Princeton College, Caldwell Co., Ky. He commenced the study of law at Potosi, Washington Co., Mo., and during the winter of 1829 and 1830 prosecuted his legal studies in Transylvania University, and in the law office of Gen. Robert Farris at St. Louis.

"In the spring of 1830 he was admitted to the bar at Belleville, St. Clair Co., Ill., and commenced the practice of law in Mt. Carmel, Wabash county.

"In 1832 Mr. Ficklin entered Capt. Jordan's company and went to the Black Hawk War, serving as quartermaster, and in the following year he was elected colonel of the militia of Wabash county, and shortly afterwards began his political career, which was one of the most honorable and brilliant enjoyed by any of his contemporaries.

"In August, 1834, he was elected to the lower house of the legislature, and was chosen by that body as state's attorney for the Wabash Circuit. In 1837 he removed to Charleston and the ensuing year represented Coles county in the legislature. In 1842 he was again elected to the legislature, and in the following year was made the member of Congress from the Wabash district, and was re-elected in the years 1844 and 1846.

"At the close of his long public career he resumed the practice of law in Charleston, but his services were considered too valuable to the public to be permitted to lead a quiet life, and in 1850 he was returned to Congress. In 1856 he was a member of the Democratic convention at Cincinnati, which nominated James Buchanan for president, and in 1860 was a member of the National convention held at Charleston, S. C. In 1864 he was a delegate to the National convention held at Chicago and which nominated George B. McClellan for president, and in 1869-70 represented the counties of Coles, Moultrie and Douglas in the State Constitutional convention. In 1878 he was elected to the house of representatives in the state legislature. He was the elector for the state at large three terms, the last was when Cleveland was elected president.

"The Hon. O. B. Ficklin was faithful in the discharge of his public duties, which were heaped upon him, and possessed the respect and esteem of his political constituents. He devoted his time and talents to the service of the state with a spirit of devotion and unselfishness. After a long and useful life, chequered by many national vicissitudes, he passed from the busy scenes of earth May 5, 1885.

"It is with pleasure that the publishers place the portrait of this lamented and honored citizen on an accompanying page, the first in the volume, a fitting place for the man represented.

"Mrs. O. B. Ficklin, the widow of the late Orlando B. Ficklin, is the daughter of Walter T. and Nancy (Lane) Colquitt, of Georgia."

Orlando Bell Ficklin, of Illinois.

The widow of Orlando B. Ficklin died 14 September, 1895. Their descendants are as follows:†

267. Walter, died in infancy.

268. Augustus W., married Nettie Highland, and died 19 February, 1876, and had one son, Augustus W., who is unmarried and lives at Charleston, Ill.

269. Orlando Bell, married Mary Wright, and died 11 February, 1894. His children were: Joseph C., of Charleston, Ill.; Mary K., who married J. J. Richey, of Champaign, Ill.; and Samuel Wright, a seaman in the U. S. Navy.

270. Alfred C., married Emma Weiss, 24 September, 1877, and died 9 August, 1903. His widow survived him and is living in Fresno county, California. Their children are: Orlando B., died 9 April, 1889; Otto W., who is unmarried and in business in Joplin, Missouri; Lizzie Colquitt, died 13 November, 1886; Walter Colquitt, living in Kerman, California; Emily Colquitt, who married Lewis C. Perley, and resides at Missoula, Montana.

271. Joseph Colquitt, married Susie Thomas and resides in Chicago. They have one son, James Roberts, who is associated with his father in business.

---

111. Joseph Ficklin, Sr., son of Jared and Elizabeth (Dunklin) Ficklin, was born in Danville, Kentucky, in 1811. In 1831 he married Eleanor Wilson Brown.‡ They lived first on a farm near Salvisa, in Mercer county, but later moved to a farm between Pleasant Hill and Harrodsburg, the former a village inhabited by the Shakers. Here he engaged

†Data concerning the descendants of Orlando B. Ficklin was furnished by Mrs. Emma Weiss Ficklin, of Kerman, Fresno Co., Calif.

‡Eleanor Wilson Brown, born 6 October, 1815, was a daughter of Wm. Brown, born 22 July, 1786, died 9 April, 1855, and wife, Nancy (Cecil) Brown, born 4 February, 1791, died 11 June, 1868, both of Mercer county, Ky. William Brown was son of Wm. Brown, senior, and Isabella Scott. Nancy Cecil was daughter of James Cecil and wife, Eleanor Wilson, who died 19 June, 1844.—From note book of Joseph Ficklin, of Columbia, Mo., 1876.

in wagon making and farming. His wife died 26 January, 1849, and is buried on her father's old farm, which is about five miles from Harrodsburg, on the Lexington Turnpike. The grave is appropriately marked. To this union were born:

*272. Joseph, Jr.
*273. Mary Ellen.
*274. Sarah A.
*275. James William.
*276. Nancy.
*277. John Cecil.
*278. Catherine. } Twins.
*279. Taylor. }

After the death of his first wife, Joseph Ficklin, in 1851, emigrated to Trenton, Missouri. Here he married, second, Mrs. Nancy Carter, a widow with two children, John and Betsy Carter. At the outbreak of the Civil War, he was living at Linneus, Missouri, where he owned a farm and general store. These were plundered by Federal soldiers in 1861. He then started a hotel at Chillicothe, Missouri, but this was confiscated, as he was a Southern sympathizer. Then, over fifty years of age, he joined the Confederate forces of General Sterling Price, and became a member of the body guard of that general, serving through the early years of the War. He died in Columbia, Missouri, 8 December, 1871, and is buried in the cemetery there. Nancy Carter Ficklin survived her husband. She and her daughter Betsy are buried in the cemetery at Colusa, California. To this union were born:†

*280. Nellie.
*281. Annie.
*282. Herbert.

112. John Ficklin, son of Jared and Elizabeth (Dunklin) Ficklin, did not marry. He died about 1875, and is buried in the cemetery at Chillicothe, Missouri.‡

---

†Data concerning this Joseph Ficklin was furnished by his daughter, Mrs. C. C. Newman, of Columbia, Mo.

‡Data concerning this John Ficklin was furnished by Nicholas F. Ficklin, of Union, Oregon.

113. Robert Ficklin, son of Jared and Elizabeth (Dunklin) Ficklin, was born in 1816. He was an intelligent and prosperous farmer, living at Pleasant Ridge in Davies county, Kentucky. He died about 1893. He married Sarah Shortridge. She died in 1897. Their children were:†

    *283. William J.
    *284. Mary.
    *285. Robert, Jr.
    *286. Narcissa.
    *287. Florence.
    *288. Susan.
    *289. Sarah.

114. William T. Ficklin, son of Jared and Elizabeth (Dunklin) Ficklin, was born in Danville, Kentucky, 6 April, 1818. He married Fetna Ann Fleece; they emigrated to Trenton, Missouri, in 1852, and in 1864, crossed the plains and mountains with an ox team and settled in Union county, Oregon. William Ficklin died in 1889, his wife survived him and died in Baker City, Oregon, in August, 1899. Both are buried at Union. Their children were:‡

    *290. Robert.
    *291. Nicholas F.
    *292. John C.
    *293. Mary W.
    *294. Joseph. ⎫ Twins.
    *295. George D. ⎭
    *296. Jared.
    *297. Sandusky D.
    *298. Thomas.

115. Sarah Ann Ficklin, daughter of Jared and Elizabeth (Dunklin) Ficklin, married Dr. Clinton Bluford Fleece, brother of Fetna Ann Fleece, mentioned above (see No. 114). Sarah Fleece died in 1845, a few

---

†Data concerning this Robert Ficklin was furnished by his daughter, Mrs. Joseph Ficklin, of Diamond, Washington.

‡Data concerning this William T. Ficklin was furnished by his son, Nicholas F. Ficklin, of Union, Oregon.

74

weeks after the birth of her youngest son.   She is buried in Kentucky.
Their children were:†
      *299. John Caldwell Fleece.
      *300. Elizabeth H. Fleece.
      *301. Wm. Hamilton Fleece.
[Dr. Fleece, born 2 January, 1818, was subsequently married three times.
He moved to Trenton, Missouri, in 1858, and to North Salem, Indiana,
in 1863, where he died 28 October, 1885.]

123.   Jarrett Ficklin, son of William and Frances (Walker) Ficklin, died
many years ago.   He married Marah Scott and lived at Jeffersonville,
Montgomery county, Kentucky.   His widow is still living at that place.
Their children were:
      302. John William, who married Miss Lizzie Borders.
      303. Charles Scott, married Miss Ann Adams, and resides at
           Salem, Oregon.
      304. James Thomas, is dead; he married Sarah Kelley and
           lived at Jeffersonville, Ky.
      305. A. Walker, married Julia Barnes, and lives in Jefferson-
           ville, Kentucky.
      306. Fannie, married E. S. Congleton, and lives at Camargo,
           Kentucky.
In addition to the above they had the following four sons, who are
not married, and are living in Montgomery county, Kentucky.
      307. Jarrett Price.
      308. Joseph McClellan.
      309. Laban F.
      310. Henry Clay.

124.   Ellen Ficklin, daughter of Thomas and Mary (Goodloe) Ficklin, married James M. Graham—being his second wife.   They had four children,
names not known.

†Data concerning this Sarah Ficklin was furnished by her son, Wm. H. Fleece, of Portland, Oregon,
and her granddaughter, Mrs. Mollie F. Robbins, of Warmsprings, Oregon.

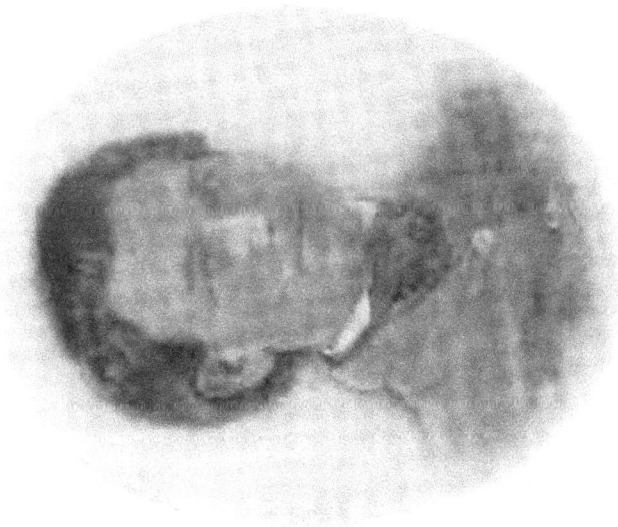

Colonel John Ficklin, of Bath County, Kentucky, and Wife, Sarah A. (Graham) Ficklin.
(From photographs taken in 1848.)

125. John Ficklin, son of Thomas and Mary (Goodloe) Ficklin, was born in Bath county, Kentucky, in 1822. He was a soldier in the War with Mexico, being in the battle of Buena Vista, 23 February, 1847, and others. In 1848 he married Sarah A. Graham, daughter of James M. Graham, mentioned above (see No. 124). In 1857-59 he represented Bath county in the legislature. When the Civil War broke out he assisted in organizing the Confederate Army in Kentucky, and was at one time commander of all the forces in eastern Kentucky. He afterwards raised a regiment of which he was colonel, and which bore his name. With this he served till the close of the War. In 1868 he was elected sheriff of Bath county, but being disqualified by Act of Congress, resigned—his oldest son, James G., being elected in his stead. In 1882 he emigrated with his family to Clinton county, Missouri, where he died 22 February, 1893. To this couple were born fifteen children, ten of whom grew to manhood or womanhood:

    *311. James G.
    *312. Thomas.
    *313. Margaret M.
    *314. Ellen.
    *315. John.
    *316. Sarah.
    *317. Robert Lee.
    *318. Stuart.
    *319. Henry Walker.
    *320. Kate.

126. James Price Ficklin, son of Thomas and Mary (Goodloe) Ficklin, was born in Kentucky. He married, first, Miss Margaret Berry. To this union no children were born. He married, second, Miss M. A. Dawson. One child was born:

    321. Margaret, born 17 October, 1846; died 31 August, 1868.

He married, third, Margaret Myers. To them were born five sons, one dying in infancy unnamed. This family moved to Hill county, Texas (near Hillsboro), in 1882. James P. Ficklin died 26 January, 1901. Margaret (Myers) Ficklin died 18 May, 1904. The children were:

322. Joseph P., born 27 April, 1855; married Fannie M. Kincart, 16 December, 1894. They live at Hillsboro, Texas, and have six children: Chalmer J., born 8 November, 1895; Margaret H., born 12 October, 1896; Lucy H., born 16 August, 1898; Cora B., born 6 April, 1901; Clara Blanche, born 13 May, 1903; Joseph Bailey, born 22 December, 1906, died 4 March, 1907.

323. Thomas, born 4 May, 1857; died 2 October, 1857.

324. Elias J., born 11 November, 1858; married Miss Clara ———— 24 December, 1883. They live at Hillsboro and have eight children: Margaret, born 25 July, 1885, died 3 February, 1886; Mattie Earle, born 7 August, 1887; J. Milton, born 10 February, 1890; Etta Jess, born 16 July, 1892; Lucile, born 9 November, 1895, died 14 December, 1895; James Bryan, born 27 January, 1897, died 18 May, 1903; Nina May, born 30 May, 1900, died 12 October, 1900; Charles Benson, born 16 November, 1901.

325. William, born 31 December, 1859; died 3 November, 1861.

127. Newton Ficklin, son of Thomas and Mary (Goodloe) Ficklin, died young.

128. Joseph Ficklin, son of Thomas and Mary (Goodloe) Ficklin, crossed the plains to California in 1849, and died there hunting gold.

129. Thomas Ficklin, son of Thomas and Mary (Goodloe) Ficklin, died at Matamoras, during the war with Mexico, while a soldier in the Army of General Zachary Taylor.

130. Madison Ficklin, son of Thomas and Mary (Goodloe) Ficklin, died young.

————————

143. Anthony Killgore, son of Charles and Lucy (Ficklin) Killgore, was born in Mason county, Kentucky, 29 October, 1813. Married Mary

Graves 11 February, 1841.   Died in Clinton county, Missouri, 4 October, 1876.   They had a son:

> 326.   John Barker Killgore, who lived for a number of years in Denver, but now resides at Oktaha, Oklahoma.

144.   Julia Ann Killgore, daughter of Charles and Lucy (Ficklin) Killgore, was born 5 August, 1815.

145.   John Ficklin Killgore, son of Charles and Lucy (Ficklin) Killgore, was born in Mason county, Kentucky, 2 November, 1817.   Married Harriet Payton, 8 October, 1840.

146.   Robert James Killgore, son of Charles and Lucy (Ficklin) Killgore, was born in Mason county, Kentucky, 29 February, 1820; married Alice Van Syckle, 3 January, 1843.   He resided at Flemington, N. J., where he was editor and proprietor of the "Hunterdon County Democrat."   He died 29 September, 1898.   They have a son, Anthony Killgore, who resides at Flemington, and is engaged in journalism; and a daughter, Mrs. Charles H. Chapman.

147.   Joseph Henry Killgore, son of Charles and Lucy (Ficklin) Killgore, was born 29 May, 1822; died 13 August, 1824.

148.   Lucy Killgore, daughter of Charles and Lucy (Ficklin) Killgore, was born 5 February, 1824; died 7 June, 1839.

149.   Angelina Killgore, daughter of Charles and Lucy (Ficklin) Killgore, was born in Mason county, Kentucky, 20 April, 1826; died 26 February, 1850.

150.   Melvina Killgore, daughter of Charles and Lucy (Ficklin) Killgore, was born in Mason county, Kentucky, 22 December, 1828.   Married William F. Sallee, 29 January, 1846.

151.   Charles Henry Killgore, son of Charles and Lucy (Ficklin) Killgore, was born 15 April, 1831; died 5 May, 1833.

152.   Sarah Ann Killgore, daughter of Charles and Lucy (Ficklin) Killgore, was born in Mason county, Kentucky, 11 June, 1833.   She married Joseph Burton 22 June, 1858, and lived near Washington, Kentucky, where Mr. Burton died 15 August, 1867, leaving one child, a daughter, who afterwards married Theodore Myers of St. Louis, a leading whole-

sale druggist. Sarah Ann Burton married, second, Porter M. Austin, in April, 1871. Mr. Austin was a lawyer of Kansas City, Missouri, and here they lived for many years, but subsequently living in Oakland, California, St. Louis and Savannah, Georgia, until a few years ago, when they moved to Brooklyn, New York, where Mr. Austin had an extensive insurance business. Sarah Ann Austin died in Brooklyn 21 May, 1909, and is buried in Kansas City, beside her daughter, Mrs. Myers.

153.   Judith Ellen Killgore, daughter of Charles and Lucy (Ficklin) Killgore, was born 21 April, 1836; died 7 February, 1837.

---

154.   Anna Hopkinson Ficklin, daughter of Robert and Alice (Cox) Ficklin, was born 20 July, 1842. Married Capt. James A. Lee, of the Federal Army, 31 May, 1866. Captain Lee died 14 September, 1870, leaving no children. His widow is living in Maysville, Kentucky.

155.   Caroline Kenyon Ficklin, daughter of Robert and Alice (Cox) Ficklin, was born 2 October, 1843, and died 6 September, 1844.

156.   Allen Bruce Ficklin, son of Robert and Alice (Cox) Ficklin, was born 28 January, 1845, and died 4 July, 1846.

157.   Alice Ficklin, daughter of Robert and Alice (Cox) Ficklin, was born in the old homestead in West Fourth Street in Maysville, 21 August, 1846. Here she died 8 March, 1908. Her untimely death was caused by the severe nervous shock resulting from the sudden death of her brother, Robert, which occurred a few days previous. She was never married. She took a lively interest in family history and contributed much valuable information used in this book. She is buried in the Maysville cemetery.

158.   Lucy Adelaide Ficklin, daughter of Robert and Alice (Cox) Ficklin, was born 16 June, 1848. Married William C. Shackleford 16 June, 1870. They live in Chicago, and to them were born three daughters:

>   327.   Anna Chambers Shackleford was born 30 April, 1871, and lives with her parents in Chicago.
>
>   328.   Alice Lee Shackleford was born 18 January, 1877.
>
>   329.   Carrie Keith Shackleford, born 23 February, 1880; died 1 June, 1895.

159. Robert Ficklin, son of Robert and Alice (Cox) Ficklin, was born 13 March, 1850, and married Imogene McLaughlin, daughter of C. A. McLaughlin of Covington, Kentucky, 18 January, 1877. He was in young manhood associated with his father in the dry goods business in Maysville. He later engaged in traffic on the Ohio river, and afterwards was agent for the Louisville and Nashville railroad at Maysville. He died 5 February, 1908, and is buried in the Maysville cemetery. His two children are:

> 330. Julia Burton, born 31 August, 1878. Married Dr. S. R. Harover, and lives at Maysville. They have three children: Robert Ficklin Harover, born 31 July, 1900; Eliza Lee Harover, born 1 September, 1901, died May, 1911; Samuel R. Harover, born 28 January, 1904.

> 331. Imogene Kenyon, born 4 November, 1892, married Raymond D. Ross, and lives in Covington, Kentucky. They have two children: Raymond Dudley Ross, Jr., born 20 August, 1907; Jane Hamilton Ross, born March, 1911.

160. Horatio Ficklin, son of Robert and Alice (Cox) Ficklin, was born 3 December, 1851, is a bachelor and is in business in Maysville. He resides at the old homestead in West Fourth Street, which has been the family residence for over seventy years.

---

161. Christopher DeAtley Ficklin, son of Famous, was born in 1798 and died about 1850. He lived in Richmond county, Virginia. He married, first, Miss Louisa Franklin. Their children are all dead, and were as follows:

> *332. William.
> *333. Thomas Dorsey.
> *334. Virginia.

Christopher DeAtley Ficklin married, second, Mary Wright, daughter of Capt. Geo. M. Wright (1812) and Catherine Pope Sand-

ford, and was a great-granddaughter of Arthur Middleton, signer of the
Declaration of Independence. She died in 1899, aged 83. There were
thirteen children by this marriage, of whom two are living:

    *335. Eugene D.

    *336. Theodore H.

---

165. John Fielding Ficklen, son of James Grant and Katherine (Davenport)
Ficklen, lived, first, at Fredericksburg, Virginia. He married 2 November,
1847, his first cousin, Sarah Anne Slaughter (No. 210), daughter of
William and Harriet (Ficklen) Slaughter, who was born at the "Hermitage" in Culpeper county, 26 July, 1824. This family, after 1860, resided at "Oaklawn" in Danville, Virginia. John Fielding was a banker.
He died 8 February, 1872; his wife 24 June, 1894. Both are buried
in Danville. There were seven children, as follows:

    337. James William, born 10 August, 1848; did not marry;
           died 17 October, 1878.

    338. Harriet, born 7 December, 1849; died 30 May, 1862.

    339. Warren Slaughter, born 17 March, 1851; married Lucy
           Balling Langhorne of Lynchburg, 23 July, 1879.
           They lived in Danville. She died in 1883. He died
           7 January, 1902. They had one son, John Lang-
           horne, born 14 September, 1883. Warren Slaughter
           Ficklen married, second, Molly Bandy of Roanoke,
           Virginia. To this union were born no children.

    340. Sarah Campbell, born 5 August, 1853; died 30 May,
           1862.

    341. John Davenport, born 11 December, 1859; married
           Mary V. Lyon of Atlanta, Georgia, 9 June, 1892.
           They lived in Danville. He died 5 August, 1894,
           leaving one son: John Davenport, Jr., born 1893.

    342. Harry Campbell, frequently mentioned elsewhere in this
           volume, is a graduate of the University of Virginia,
           is not married, and is one of the most prominent young
           business men in Danville.

Harry Campbell Ficklen, of Danville, Virginia.

"Though branches ever grow apart,
When from the parent stem they start,
They touch again in broadening reach,
And leaves will whisper each to each."
                    —H. C. F., 1910.

343. Catherine Nelson, was married to Alexander Humphrey Robinson of Louisville, Kentucky, 9 June, 1891. They have one son, Goldsborough Robinson, born 1895.

166. Ellen Douglas Ficklen, daughter of James Grant and Katherine (Davenport) Ficklen, married her cousin, Charles Gideon Brown, son of Wm. and Sarah Ficklen Brown (No. 202); both are buried in Charlottesville, Virginia. Their children were:

344. Charles Brown, never married.
345. James Brown, never married.
346. Kate D. Brown, who lives in Norfolk, Virginia.

167. James Burwell Ficklen, son of James Grant, and Katherine (Davenport) Ficklen. The following biography was prepared by his daughter, Mrs. Kate Ficklen Marshall, of Lynchburg, Virginia, largely from newspaper cuttings:

"James Burwell Ficklen was born at 'Belleville,' near Winchester, Virginia, October 1, 1831. His father died when he was eleven years of age, whereupon he and his widowed mother and several sisters moved to Winchester. He was first employed at the dry goods house of John Sherrard. He displayed rare business talent and was a zealous student of literature. In 1850 he moved to Fredericksburg and became a member of the dry goods firm of Ficklen, Halmer & Wallace. Continuing in this prosperous business till 1855, when seeking a larger field, he established in Richmond the dry goods firm of Ficklen & Watkins, which continued till the outbreak of the Civil War. July 11, 1860, he married Miss Fannie A. Pannill of Pittsylvania county, Virginia.

"He was a member of the Richmond Howitzers, commanded by Maj. Geo. W. Randolph, and was on duty at Harper's Ferry and Charlestown during the raid and capture of John Brown. In 1863 he purchased a large plantation on James river in Buckingham county, known as the 'Red House Plantation,' and was detailed to raise supplies for the Confederacy. Here later, after retirement from active business, he had the opportunity to indulge his natural taste and devoted much of his time to literary pursuits and collected a large library.

"He represented Buckingham county in the Virginia legislature for many years and his equal in debate could not be found. The Richmond 'Whig' of February 16, 1878, in editorial comment on one of his speeches before the house of delegates, speaks of it as one of the finest ever delivered in the Virginia house. In 1876 he was delegate at large from Virginia to the National Democratic convention at St. Louis, at which he seconded the nomination of Samuel J. Tilden for president, using the words: 'Give us Tilden and we will give you the electoral vote from the Potomac to the Rio Grande.' Whereupon Flournoy of South Carolina caught up the expression and shouted: 'Give us Tilden and we will give you the solid South.' This is claimed to be the origin of the expression 'Solid South.' In 1878 he was commissioner from Virginia to the Paris Exposition.

"The strain of public life now began to tell on his naturally delicate constitution, and on January 31, 1883, this noble life came to an untimely end. He is buried in the Presbyterian churchyard at New Canton, near his old home in Buckingham."

His children are:

347. Kate Fielding, married 24 June, 1885, Mr. Hunter Marshall of Lynchburg, Virginia. Their home is at Lynchburg, but they spend much of their time in Florida. Mrs. Marshall has contributed much valuable information used in this book. They have one son: Hunter Marshall, Jr., who is at present a law student at the University of Virginia.

348. Samuel Pannill, married Elise Daviette Carbell. He holds the enviable record of being the leading representative in the United States of the Travelers' Insurance Company (Life). He lives in Washington, D. C., and has two children: Daviette Carbell and Holmes.

349. Maria Louisa, is dead—never married.

350. Elizabeth Stuart, married Holman Myers, who died leaving no children. His widow resides in Huntington, West Virginia.

James Burwell Ficklen, of Buckingham County, Virginia.

351. Edward Bancroft, married Elmira Ward Skinner, and lives at Greenville, North Carolina. They have two children: James Skinner and Edward Bancroft, Jr.

352. Anne Eliza, married Gilbert Carey Jeter. He died leaving three children. His widow lives in Bedford City, Virginia. Their children are: Fielding Ficklen Jeter, Frances Louisa Jeter, Gilbert Carey Jeter.

353. Ellen Douglas, married Louis Chesterfield Arthur, and lives in Greenville, North Carolina. They have six children: James Ficklen Arthur, Louis Chesterfield Arthur, Jr., Ellen Douglas Arthur, Virginia Laughinghouse Arthur, Nannie Russel Arthur, Robert Bruce Arthur.

354. James B., is pastor of the Inman Park Presbyterian church, of Atlanta, Georgia. He married Miss Ruth Vannerson, of Atlanta, 31 July, 1911.

355. Willie Letcher, married Geo. B. Hughes, who died leaving no children. She married, second, Bennett Wesley Moseley. They live in Greenville, North Carolina, and have two children: Frances Venable Moseley and Bennett W. Moseley, Jr.

168. Nannie Ficklen, daughter of James Grant and Katherine (Davenport) Ficklen, married S. S. Howison in Alexandria, both are buried at Fredericksburg, Virginia. They had seventeen children, all of whom died in infancy, except six.

356. Marion L. Howison, who married Dr. W. W. Smith, of the Randolph Macon College at Lynchburg. Dr. Smith is one of the foremost educators of the South.

357. Allan M. Howison, who married Annie Hotchkiss. They live in Staunton, Virginia, and have one child, Nellie M. Howison.

358. James F. Howison, who married, first, Alice Jackson. They had six children: Marion L., Alice, Telka, James, Nancy and Jackson. He married, second,

Mary Anderson of Richmond, Virginia. They have one child and reside in Memphis, Tennessee.

359. Susie D. Howison, who never married.

360. Robert C. Howison, who is not married and lives in Richmond, Virginia:

361. Nannie Howison, who married Joseph Riddick. They have several small children and live at Wytheville, Virginia.

169. Susan Matthews Ficklen, daughter of James Grant, and Katherine (Davenport) Ficklen, married 28 May, 1868, Dr. Edward Jaquelin Harrison of Cumberland county, Virginia, who was surgeon in the Confederate Army for four years, and stationed at the Chimbarazo hospital, Richmond. They are living in Kingston, New York. Their children are:

362. James Burwell Harrison, never married.

363. Henry Jaquelin Harrison, died, aged 29. Never married.

364. Bessie Ambler Harrison, married James Overton Winston, of Louisa county, Virginia, who was constructing engineer of the famous Wachusett dam near Boston, Massachusetts, and is now engaged on the Oshokan dam in the Catskills for supplying New York City with water. They live at Kingston, New York. Their children are: William Alexander Winston, James Overton Winston, Jr., Jaquelin Ambler Winston, Randolph Harrison Winston.

365. Katharine Davenport Harrison is not married and lives with her parents at Kingston, New York.

170. Rebecca Davenport Ficklen, daughter of James Grant and Katherine (Davenport) Ficklen, married A. H. Miller, and lived, first, in Baltimore, but later moved to Saltville, Virginia. She is still living. They had five children:

366. Ada Miller, not married.

367. Henry Miller, not married.

368. Nannie Miller, married John McGavock. They have one child and live at Arlington, Virginia.

369. Elizabeth Miller, married Julian S. Gertchins. They have no children and reside at Saltville, Virginia.

370. Ellen Miller, married Henry Jacocke. They have one child and live at Saltville, Virginia.

171. Elizabeth Ficklen, daughter of George and Fannie (Kennon) Ficklen, married Thomas Hill of Culpeper county, Virginia, in 1835. They had four children:

371. Fentres Hill, married A. C. Jennings. Their children are: (a) Thomas C. Jennings, who lives at Wray, Colorado, is judge of the Yuma county court, and has two children, Mary and Bernard. (b) Henry Jennings, married Mattie Burgess, lives at Baltimore, and has three children: Lulu, Caroll and Burgess. (c) Elizabeth Jennings, died not married. (d) Lulu Jennings, married Frank Brown and died, leaving one child: Eloise. (e) Guy Jennings, married Minnie Bowen and has two children: Lillie and Clareta. (f) G. Powell Jennings, married Sarah Watson and lives at Durango, Mexico. They have two children: William Powell and Hazel Hill.

372. G. Powell Hill, married Mattie McVeigh, and has four children: (a) I. Newton Hill, who died not married. (b) Malvern Hill, married Etta Jones, lives at Richmond, Virginia, and has one child. (c) Lilly A. Hill, died not married. (d) Charles B. Hill, lives somewhere in the West. He first married Miss Mitchell, and had a son and daughter. His first wife is dead and he has married again.

373. William A. Hill, married Fannie P. ———, and died without issue.

374. Louisa V. Hill, is not married, and lives at Culpeper, Virginia.

172. Harriet Ficklen, daughter of George and Fannie (Kennon) Ficklen, married J. Lawrence Stringfellow, and lives in Culpeper, Virginia. They have two sons:

      375. Thornton Stringfellow, who married Cora Ewing.

      376. Geo. Ficklen Stringfellow, married, first, Elizabeth Spindle, no children; second, Ellen Summerville, and had one son; third, married Mary McMullen, and had two children.

173. Fannie M. Ficklen, daughter of George and Fannie (Kennon) Ficklen, married Dr. A. J. Coons, in 1846. They lived in St. Louis and had three daughters:

      377. Fanny Coons, married Spottswood Lomax and has several children.

      378. Fanny Ficklen Coons, married Rev. McKay and lives at Omaha. They have three children.

      379. Laura Coons.

174. Mary Virginia Ficklen, daughter of George and Fannie (Kennon) Ficklen, married Langdon C. Major. They live in Culpeper and have two children:

      380. George Ficklen Major, married Ida P. English and lives in Culpeper, Virginia. They have two children: Nellie L. Major, who married L. W. Spellhouse, and L. Cave Major.

      381. Lizzie Frances Major, who lives at Lakota, Virginia.

175. Laura Ficklen, daughter of George and Fannie (Kennon) Ficklen, married J. Mortimer Spindle, and died in early life. They had one child, a daughter, who married William Major, and has two children, Hattie and Lizzie, who are living in Culpeper county.

176. Joseph E. Ficklen, son of George and Fannie (Kennon) Ficklen, married Fannie Mayo Braxton of Fredericksburg. He was a major in the 51st Virginia Infantry, C. S. A. They live in Culpeper and have three children:

      382. George Edward, who is married and has two sons. He lives at Orange, Virginia.

383. Elizabeth Mayo, who married W. H. Landon, and lives at Newport News, Virginia. They have four children.

384. Carter Braxton, who married Miss Michaux of Richmond, Virginia. They live in Brooklyn, and have no children.

177. Sarah Ficklen, daughter of George and Fannie (Kennon) Ficklen, died young.

178. Louisa Ficklen, daughter of George and Fannie (Kennon) Ficklen, died young.

179. Georgia Ficklen, daughter of George and Fannie (Kennon) Ficklen, died at age of 16 while at school in St. Louis, and on a visit to her sister, Fannie.

180. Lucy Ficklen, daughter of George and Fanny (Kennon) Ficklen, died not married.

181. Joseph Burwell Ficklen, son of Joseph Burwell and Anne (Fitzhugh) Ficklen, married, first, Miss Carry Gordon Hall of Fredericksburg, and had one daughter:

385. Carry Stuart, who married Hoomes Johnston, and lives in Fredericksburg, Virginia.

He married, second, Miss Ellen Coskie London, of Richmond, Virginia. He lived and died in Fredericksburg. To this second union was born one son:

386. Joseph Burwell.

182. Edmonia Fitzhugh Ficklen, daughter of Joseph Burwell and Anne (Fitzhugh) Ficklen, married James Parke Corbin of Fredericksburg. He died leaving no children.

183. Nannie Ficklen, daughter of Joseph Burwell and Anne (Fitzhugh) Ficklen, married Daniel Murray Lee of Stafford county, Virginia, brother of Gen. Fitzhugh Lee, and nephew of Gen. Robert E. Lee. They live at Fredericksburg and have six children, none married:

387. Murray Lee.

388. Joseph Burwell Lee.
389. Edmonia Fitzhugh Lee.
390. Mary Custis Lee.
391. Sidney Smith Lee.
392. Harry Fitzhugh Lee.

184. William Fitzhugh Ficklen, son of Joseph Burwell and Anne (Fitzhugh) Ficklen, resides at the old family homestead "Belmont," in Stafford county, near Falmouth.   He formerly operated the Bridgewater Mills at Fredericksburg.   He married Miss Julia Belle Stansbury of "Snowdon," Spottsylvania county.   They have nine children, none married except the oldest:

393. Belle, who married Dr. Owen and resides at Black Walnut, Halifax county, Virginia.   They have two children.
394. Joseph Burwell.
395. Anne Eliza.
396. Elize.
397. Stansbury.
398. William Fitzhugh, Jr.
399. Contee.
400. Virginia.
401. Conway.

185. George Ficklen, son of Joseph Burwell and Anne (Fitzhugh) Ficklen, died not married and is buried at Fredericksburg.

186. John Rose Ficklen, son of Joseph Burwell and Anne (Fitzhugh) Ficklen, was born in "Belmont," Falmouth, Virginia, 14 December, 1858.   He graduated from the University of Virginia in 1879, and in the same year was made Professor of History in Tulane University, New Orleans, which position he held with honor to himself and the institution till his death, which occurred at Chautauqua, New York, 3 August, 1907. In December, 1886, he married Miss Bessie Mason Alexander, daughter of General E. P. Alexander, of Georgia.   Among his valuable contributions to historical literature may be noted his "Constitutional History of Louisiana," and "History of Reconstruction in Louisiana."   With Grace

King he was author of "Louisiana History," and "Stories from Louisiana History," and, with Alice Fortier, author of "Mexico and Central America," etc.

He is buried at Fredericksburg, Virginia. His widow, who is also widely known for her literary contributions, is living in New Orleans. Their children are:

    402. Porter Alexander, born 25 October, 1887; graduated (B.S.), Tulane University, 1907, (M.D.) 1911. He married Beatrice Reta Kennedy, 5 September, 1911.

    403. Elizabeth Fitzhugh, born 11 May, 1890; graduated (B.S. Domestic Science), Teachers' College, Columbia University, New York.

---

187. James Ficklen and (188) Samuel Ficklen, sons of Fielding and Frances (Wingfield) Ficklen, died in childhood.

189. Joseph Burwell Ficklen, son of Fielding and Frances (Wingfield) Ficklen, was, like his father, a physician. He married Miss Julia Weems and lived at Washington, Georgia, where he died about 1893, leaving no children. His widow lives in Washington, Georgia.

190. Elizabeth Ficklen, daughter of Fielding and Frances (Wingfield) Ficklen, married Rev. James P. Boyce, of Charleston, South Carolina, who was largely instrumental in establishing the Baptist Theological Seminary, first in Greenville, South Carolina, and afterwards moving it to Louisville, Kentucky. Both are dead. They left three daughters, who are living in Washington, D. C.:

    404. Elizabeth Ficklen Boyce.
    405. Frances Wingfield Boyce.
    406. Lucy Garnsey Boyce.

191. Georgia Ficklen, daughter of Fielding and Frances (Wingfield) Ficklen, married Rev. Morgan Callaway, a Methodist minister and vice-president of Emory College at Oxford, Georgia. Both are dead. They had one child, a daughter:

    407. Hattie Callaway, who is also dead.

192. Sarah Ficklen, daughter of Fielding and Frances (Wingfield) Ficklen, married Judge David A. Vason of Albany, Georgia, and died leaving no children.

193. Mary Ficklen, daughter of Fielding and Frances (Wingfield) Ficklen, married Dr. A. J. Almond, and lived for many years in Bedford county, Virginia, afterwards moving to Atlanta, Georgia, where she died, leaving one son:

    408. George Almond, who is living in Atlanta.

194. William Ficklen, son of Fielding and Frances (Wingfield) Ficklen, married Julia Anthony, of Washington, Georgia. Both are dead. They had ten children:

    409. Marion, who died in young manhood.

    410. Georgia, who married Rev. A. J. Shankle, a Methodist minister, and resides at Ruston, La. They have two small boys: Warren Shankle and Arthur Shankle.

    411. Julia, married Thomas Pope and resides at Kirkwood, near Atlanta, Georgia. They have no children.

    412. James, is married and has several children. He lives at Fitzgerald, Georgia.

    413. Burwell, married Miss McAvoy, of Wilkes county, Georgia, and moved to Garner, Texas. They have one child.

    414. Lizzie, married John T. Lowe, and resides at Kirkwood, Georgia. They have two sons, one is Thomas Pope Lowe.

    415. Claudia, lives with her sister, Mrs. Shankle, at Ruston, Louisiana.

    416. John, died young.

    417. Susie, died young.

    418. Bettie, died young.

195. John Ficklen, son of Fielding and Frances (Wingfield) Ficklen, married Eliza Battle, of Washington, Georgia, and moved to Waco, Texas. Both are dead. They left two sons:

    419. John Fielding.

    420. Irvin.

196. Ella Ficklen, daughter of Fielding and Frances (Wingfield) Ficklen, married J. J. Griffin, who is now dead. The widow is living in Atlanta. They had four children:

    421. Fielding Griffin, who died in infancy.

    422. Marie Griffin, who married Phillip Townsend and died about six years ago, leaving one child, who is living with its grandmother.

    423. Hattie Claire Griffin, and

    424. Louise Griffin, are living with their widowed mother.

197. Boyce Ficklen, son of Fielding and Frances (Wingfield) Ficklen, married Mary Hill and resides in Washington, Georgia. They have five children:

    425. Fielding, married Celeste Bounds and has three small children: Emmie, Fielding, Jr., and Mary Rembert.

    426. Nannielu, married Grier Martin and lives at Clarkston, Georgia. They have two little boys: Robert Grier Martin and Boyce Martin.

    427. Emmie, lives with her parents.

    428. Frances, lives with her parents.

    429. Boyce, Jr., married Miss Lucy Reese Dillard, 28 June, 1911, and resides at Washington, Georgia.

198. Ann Brown, daughter of William and Sarah (Ficklen) Brown, married her cousin, Geo. R. Crigler, a teacher and farmer. Their children were:

    430. Jennie Crigler, who married Lewis Botts. Their only child, Anna Ford Botts, married Charles Browning and has several small children.

    431. Roberta Crigler, who is dead. She never married.

    432. William Gideon Crigler, who married Mary Parr, and has four children: Allie Moffett, Berta (who married Ernest Browning), Hugh and Bessie.

92

199. Lucinda Brown, daughter of William and Sarah (Ficklen) Brown, married Horatio G. Moffett, a lawyer of Rappahannock county, Virginia, and for many years attorney for the commonwealth. They resided at Washington, Virginia. Their children were:

    433. Molly Moffett, who never married.

    434. William Daniel Moffett, was a captain in the Confederate Army. He married Miss Virginia Moore and died without issue 30 May, 1869. He was a lawyer of great promise.

    435. Walter Franklin Moffett, was a soldier in the Confederate Army and was killed at the Battle of Yellow Tavern, 11 May, 1864.

    436. Horatio Gates Moffett, Jr., married Ida Menefee. He has for twenty years been prosecuting attorney for Rappahannock county, Virginia. Their children are William Franklin, Mary Low (who married William Strong and has several children), Henry and Horatio Gates.

200. Henrietta Brown, daughter of William and Sarah (Ficklen) Brown, married Horatio G. Moffett, the husband of her deceased sister, Lucinda. She died childless.

201. James F. Brown, son of William and Sarah (Ficklen) Brown, married Ellen Crigler. Their children are:

    437. William R., who is not married.

    438. Bettie, who married J. W. Gully. Both are dead, leaving several children.

    439. Robert C., was a physician. He married, and died leaving one child, who is also dead.

    440. Kate,

    441. Sallie F.,

    442. Molly,

    443. Edward, are all dead. They never married.

    444. Travis Herndon, is married and has two children: Charlotte Brown and Herndon Brown.

    445. Bartow, is not married.

446. Joseph H., married Fannie Browning. Their children are: James, Edward, Josephine and Charles.

447. Frank Moffett, married Lulu Jennings and has one child.

202. Charles Gideon Brown, son of William and Sarah (Ficklen) Brown, married Ellen Douglas Ficklen (see No. 166).

203. Sarah William Brown, daughter of William and Sarah (Ficklen) Brown, was born 16 September, 1824; married John Moffett, a brother of Horatio G. Moffett, and died 21 April, 1894. They lived on their plantation at "Solitude" on Thornton river in Culpeper county, Virginia. Mr. Moffett died many years ago. Their children are:

448. William Walter Moffett, who married Jessie Mary Dudley, of Rappahannock county, Virginia, and resides at Salem, Virginia. He is judge of the Twentieth Judicial Circuit. Their children are as follows: Willie Gates, John Daniel, Fanny Dudley, Sarah Achsah, Mary Lois.

449. Sallie Ficklen Moffett, who married Rev. T. P. Brown, a Baptist minister of Culpeper county, Virginia. They have one child: John Roberts Moffett Brown.

450. Daniel A. Moffett, married Julia Booth, and resides in Baltimore, where he is a member of the wholesale dry goods firm of Tregallis Hertie & Co. They have one child: William Walter Moffett.

451. John Roberts Moffett, was a Baptist minister of distinction, and a temperance leader of influence. He was brutally assassinated in Danville, Virginia, on the night of 11 November, 1892, during a temperance campaign in that city. The Rev. S. H. Thompson, president of Scottsbury Normal College, has written an appropriate biography of this martyr. The volume consists of about 300 pages and was printed by the widow, who was Miss Pearl Bruce of Halifax county, Virginia. The children of this couple are: Daniel Bruce Moffett and Maggie E. Moffett.

204. Elizabeth Susan Slaughter, daughter of William and Harriet (Ficklen) Slaughter, was born in Culpeper county, Virginia, 21 January, 1815, and lived to be over 80 years of age. She married Reuben Garnett of Culpeper county. They lived most of their lives in Kansas City, Missouri, and are buried there. Their children were:

    452. William Garnett, who is now dead. He married Miss Elgin, and lived in Mobile, Alabama. They had two children: Charles Garnett and Albert Garnett. The latter died in childhood.

    453. Anna Garnett, married a Mr. Latimer, and lives in Oakland, California. They have several children.

    454. Emma Garnett is a teacher, and lives in Kansas City, Missouri.

    455. Ella Garnett is likewise a teacher, and lives in Kansas City, Missouri.

205. Franklin Slaughter, son of William and Harriet (Ficklen) Slaughter, was born in Culpeper county, Virginia, 18 July, 1816. He married Miss Gill and lived in Fredericksburg, Virginia, where both are buried. Their children were:

    456. Lawrence Alexander, who married Miss Mattie Lancaster, and lives in Meridian, Mississippi. They have three children: Lawrence Alexander, Jr., Richard G. (now dead) and Harriet Lucretia.

    457. Harriet, married Chas. E. Tackett, and lives at Fredericksburg, Virginia. They have no children.

    458. Franklin, Jr.,

    459. Lucretia,

    460. Jane Alexander,

    461. Etta Ruggles, never married, and are buried at Fredericksburg, Virginia.

206. Montgomery Slaughter, son of William and Harriet (Ficklen) Slaughter, was born in Culpeper county, Virginia, 21 January, 1818. He married his cousin, Eliza Jane Slaughter. Both are dead and are buried at Fredericksburg, Virginia, where they lived. He was mayor of that

city during the Civil War, and later judge of its corporation court. Their children were:

- 462. William Lane, who married Hannah Battaile Hoomes. He died without issue and is buried at Fredericksburg.
- 463. Mary Montgomery, who married Edward Lewis, and has three children: Maud Lewis, Edward Lewis, Jr., and Horace Lewis.
- 464. Fanny Scott, who is not married and is living at Fredericksburg.
- 465. Philip Mercer, who married Miss Kirsch and lives at Richmond, Virginia. They have no children.
- 466. Charles Slaughter, who is not married.
- 467. Eliza Lane, who married, first, John Berryman and had two children: Eliza Lane Berryman and John Berryman. After Mr. Berryman's death, his widow married twice—second, to a Mr. Cronie, and, third, to a Mr. Bressler.

207.   J. Warren Slaughter, son of William and Harriet (Ficklen) Slaughter, was born in Culpeper county, Virginia, 3 December, 1820. He married Miss Sallie Moore Braxton, 7 August, 1855, and lived at "Hazel Hill," in Fredericksburg, where he died 28 August, 1866. Their children were:

- 468. Carter Braxton, who died in infancy.
- 469. William Fielding, who married Jessie B. Husted and lived at Norfolk, Virginia. He died without issue.
- 470. Sallie Braxton, who married Wm. G. Ivy, of Newport News, Virginia. They had no children. She is living in Norfolk.
- 471. John Warren, who died young.
- 472. Harriet Ficklen, who died in infancy.
- 473. Elizabeth Carter, who married Emmett W. Robinson, and lives at Newport News, Virginia. They have four children: Louise Braxton Robinson, Warren Slaughter Robinson, Emmett Temple Robinson, Fielding Slaughter Robinson.

208. Albert Slaughter, son of William and Harriet (Ficklen) Slaughter, died when eight or nine years of age.

209. Sarah Anne Slaughter, daughter of William and Harriet (Ficklen) Slaughter, was born at the "Hermitage" in Culpeper county, Virginia. She married her first cousin, John Fielding Ficklen, of Fredericksburg, Virginia. For further record of this union, see No. 165.

210. Harriet Jane Slaughter, daughter of William and Harriet (Ficklen) Slaughter, was born in Culpeper county, Virginia, 29 August, 1826. She married in 1854, Dr. Franklin J. Kerfoot of Berryville, Virginia, now dead. She died 31 October, 1904. Both are buried in Berryville. Their children were:

> 474. Warren Slaughter Kerfoot, who was born in 1855, married Mary Glasscock, of Washington, D. C., and lived in Berryville, Va., where he died 17 October, 1887. They had one child, Grace Kerfoot, who in 1908 married Mr. Handy, and resides at Herndon, Virginia.
>
> 475. Wm. Francis Kerfoot, who was born 30 January, 1857, and died 11 April, 1891.
>
> 476. Harriet Ficklen Kerfoot, who died when five years of age.

211. Eliza Frances Slaughter, daughter of William and Harriet (Ficklen) Slaughter, was born 16 September, 1828, and died 4 November, 1904. She is buried in Fredericksburg, where she resided. She never married.

212. Matilda Slaughter, daughter of William, and Harriet (Ficklen) Slaughter, was born in Culpeper county, about 1836, and died at Fredericksburg, 7 October, 1907. She is buried there. She never married.

213. Joseph Fant Slaughter and (214) Joseph Fielding Slaughter, sons of William and Harriet (Ficklen) Slaughter, died in infancy.

---

215. Henrietta Reid, daughter of Dr. Mark and Eliza (Ficklen) Reid, died not married.

216. William B. Reid, son of Dr. Mark and Eliza (Ficklen) Reid, married Miss Stuart, lived in Greenbrier county, West Virginia, and died childless.

217. Virginia Pocahontas Reid, daughter of Dr. Mark and Eliza (Ficklen) Reid, died not married.

218. Sarah Reid, daughter of Dr. Mark and Eliza (Ficklen) Reid, married Dr. Caldwell and lived in Greenbrier county, West Virginia, and died in early life, leaving four children.

219. Eliza Reid, daughter of Dr. Mark and Eliza (Ficklen) Reid, married James Carberry, and resided near Georgetown, D. C. They had one son, James Carberry, Jr., who married Lizzie King.

220. Nannie B. Reid and (221) Matilda Baker Reid, daughters of Dr. Mark and Eliza (Ficklen) Reid, did not marry.

---

249. Lucy Pickett Ficklen, daughter of Daniel (II) and Achsah (Anderson) Ficklen, was born 13 December, 1835. She married Rev. John I. Rogers, and lived at Maysville, Kentucky. She died in early life. They had but one child. It died in infancy.

250. Charles Leonard Ficklen, son of Daniel (II) and Achsah (Anderson) Ficklen, was born 27 May, 1837, in Elizaville, Kentucky. He moved to Memphis, Tennessee, in 1869, and on 6 December, 1876, married Miss Lulu Young, who died in September, 1878, leaving one child:

    477. Marion, born 18 April, 1878, she is not married and is living with her stepmother in Memphis.

    Charles Leonard Ficklen married, second, Miss Leila Mitchell Johnson, 12 December, 1883. He died 30 September, 1899, leaving a splendid business record. Two children resulted from the second union:

    478. Charles Leonard, born 29 September, 1884, was one of the best known successful and respected young business men in Memphis, being manager of the insurance department of Martin & Raine. Through his industry and popularity he had made a success of his business from the start. He was but twenty-six years of

age when he succumbed to typhoid fever, 9 August, 1911. He was not married.

479. Leila Johnson, born 1 November, 1888, is living with her mother.

251. Amelia S. Ficklen, daughter of Daniel (II) and Achsah (Anderson) Ficklen, was born 28 November, 1839. She married Horace W. Miller of Owensboro, Kentucky. She died 22 July, 1893. To this union were born eight children, one of whom died in infancy, unnamed:

480. Lucy, who married O. H. Haynes, and lives at Owensboro, Kentucky. They have four children: Miller Haynes, Achsah Haynes (who married J. Stanton Cottrell, 2 June, 1910), Oliver Hart Haynes, Amelia Haynes.

481. Harmon, who married Florence Griffith of Owensboro, Kentucky, and lives at Asheville, North Carolina. They have five children: Amelia Miller, Virginia G. Miller, Daniel Miller, Florence Miller, Horace Wm. Miller.

482. Achsah Van Dyke, who married Thomas Pickett Taylor, who is in the wholesale and retail drug business in Louisville, Kentucky. They have two sons: Horace Ayres Taylor (who married Viola Whayne, 11 October, 1910), and Thomas Pickett Taylor, Jr.

483. Oscar, who died July, 1882, aged 19.

484. James, who died January, 1884, aged 19.

485. Charles, who died 14 February, 1893, aged 26.

486. Carrie, who married J. Allen Deane, and resided in Owensboro, Kentucky. She died 4 April, 1903, leaving one child, Silas Miller Deane.

252. Elizabeth Ficklen, daughter of Daniel (II) and Achsah (Anderson) Ficklen, was born 15 June, 1843, and died when three years of age.

---

272. Joseph Ficklin, Jr., son of Joseph, Sr., and Eleanor Wilson (Brown) Ficklin. An account of him appears in Appleton's Encyclopedia of

American Biography. He is given a foremost place in Lowry's History of the University of Missouri, as one of those most instrumental in the upbuilding of that institution during the stormy period following the Civil War.

The following is from Switzler's History of Boone County, Missouri (Western Historical Company, St. Louis, 1882):

"Joseph Ficklin was born in Winchester, Clark county, Kentucky, September 9, 1833; his father Joseph, Sr., was also a native of Kentucky, born in Mercer county, in 1811. When Joseph, Jr., was an infant, his father removed to a farm near the little town of Salvisa in Mercer county, and here the subject of this sketch learned to read and write. At Salvisa also he obtained his first mathematical knowledge, learning the multiplication table from the back part of an old copy book. This was before he was eight years of age. In 1841 Mr. Ficklin, Sr., removed to another farm between Pleasant Hill and Harrodsburg, the former a village inhabited by the Shakers. On this farm Joseph lived till he was eighteen years of age, employing his time at farm work and at labor in his father's wagon shop. He became a good wagon maker for one of his years. Meanwhile all of his leisure time had been devoted to the acquirement of an education, a cherished object with him, and one to be pursued under difficulties. His father was poor and had a large family to support, and the path of a poor man was not a pleasant one in Kentucky in that day. But by the time 'Joe' Ficklin was seventeen years of age, he had, almost unaided, completed common arithmetic, made some progress in Latin, and had begun the study of Davies' Elementary Algebra.

"In the autumn of 1851, the Senior Ficklin removed from Kentucky to Grundy county, Missouri. Joseph accompanied the family to St. Louis, and then went down the river to New Madrid, where he taught his first school. In February, 1852, he returned to Kentucky, and lived with his grandfather (Brown), where he had the opportunity of attending a good school until in September, 1853. Up to this period he had studied, if not mastered, algebra, geometry, trigonometry, surveying, Cæsar, Virgil, Horace, and had made some progress in Greek. He bought his books with money paid him by his grandfather for work done; the generous old gentleman charged him nothing for his board. September 18, 1853, he came to Trenton, Grundy county, Missouri, where his father then lived. Here he borrowed money and went to the old Masonic College, at Lexington, entering the sophomore class in all departments. At the close of the sophomore year his funds became exhausted, and, unable to procure more, he was reluctantly compelled to leave college, which he never after attended as a student. Subsequently, however, it conferred on him the degree of Bachelor of Arts.

"In the fall of 1854, he began teaching in the high school at Trenton, as principal. One of the trustees of the school, Mr. James Terrill, did not look with much favor on the selection of Mr. Ficklin. 'I prefer a married man,' said Mr. Terrill, 'I have two daughters who will attend the school, and I prefer that they be taught by one of mature years, settled in life. This Mr. Ficklin is a single man, and will be falling in love with one of his young lady pupils one of these days.' Mr. Terrill's worst fears were afterwards realized: Mr. Ficklin *did* conceive the tender passion for one of his young lady pupils, who was Miss Penelope Terrill,† daughter of the prophetic trustee himself! Who says there are no such sensations as premonitions of danger? Mr. and Mrs. Ficklin were married 3 March, 1856. Mrs. Ficklin was a native of Howard county, Missouri, born 10 October, 1837.

"In 1859 Prof. Ficklin accepted the chair of mathematics in Bloomington Female College, Illinois. He did not remain here long, however, and the early spring of the following year returned to Missouri. In the autumn of 1860 he took charge of the public school at Linneus, Linn county, Missouri. At the close of the term, he opened a select school, but the Civil War breaking out and continuing while he taught, his school and his income were comparatively small.

"In September, 1864, he left Linneus to accept the chair of mathematics in the Christian Female College, at Columbia. About this time a similar position was tendered him in Eminence College, Kentucky. Prof. Ficklin had been in Columbia about one year when the professorship of mathematics in the State University became vacant. Meantime

†Penelope Terrill was a descendant of William Tyrrell, who settled in New Kent county, Virginia, in 1667. This is set forth on pages 26-27 of the "Genealogy of Richmond and William Tyrrell, who Settled in Virginia in the Seventeenth Century," by Joseph Henry Tyrrell, Castleknock, Twickenham, October, 1910. In 1904 the same author published his excellent "History of the Tyrrells," which gives an account of this splendid old Norman-English family from ancient times.

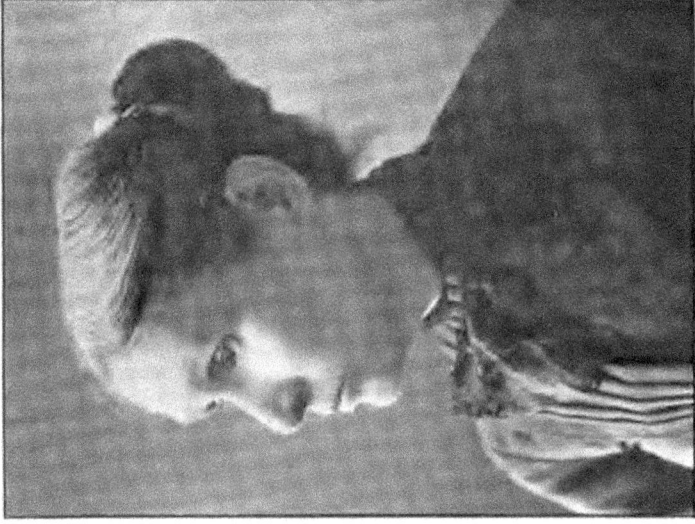

Professor Joseph Ficklin, of University of Missouri, Columbia, Mo., and Wife, Penelope (Terrill) Ficklin.

he had been a contributor to mathematical departments of certain scientific journals, and had published solutions of certain intricate and difficult problems, which indicated superior and profound knowledge of mathematics on his part. One of these solutions fell under the observation of President Lathrop of the University. At a meeting of the officers of that institution to fill the vacancy in the mathematical chair, Dr. Lathrop said: 'Gentlemen, are you aware that we have the very man for the place right here in Columbia? That little fellow over at Christian College is the very man we want.' This led to investigation and the election of Prof. Ficklin to the professorship of mathematics in Missouri's greatest, noblest school.

"In 1874 the 'little fellow from Christian College' received the degree of Ph.D. from the University of Wisconsin. The University of Missouri had previously made him *Artium Magister*, or Master of Arts. (In 1884 the University of Wisconsin conferred upon him the degree of Doctor of Laws.) He is a Fellow of the American Association for the Advancement of Science, whose sessions he attends when practicable, and before which organization he has read valuable papers. In 1869 he assisted Prof. Snell of Amherst College in a revision of the college edition of Olmsted's Natural Philosophy, himself revising the entire mathematical portion of the work. In 1874 he published, through Ivison, Blakeman, Taylor & Co., New York, his complete algebra and algebraic problems; also a key to both works. In 1881 appeared from the house of A. S. Barnes & Co., New York, Ficklin's Primary Arithmetic, Ficklin's Practical Arithmetic, Ficklin's National Arithmetic and Ficklin's Elements of Algebra, with keys to the last three named. Prof. Ficklin's mathematical works have been well received throughout the country, and his fame as a scientist is already well established in the United States, and in Europe. No man ought to be more proud of reputation honestly gained, and fairly maintained, than this 'little fellow,' and yet no man is less so. The La Place of Missouri, he is 'as common as an old shoe,' as unassuming and accessible as if he were still a country wagon-maker instead of a learned professor and philosopher, and as genial and agreeable a companion as you shall meet anywhere, 'on a summer's day.'

"Professor Ficklin has been a member of the Christian church for twenty-six years. He is a member of the Masonic order. In politics he takes no very active part, but votes the Democratic ticket when he goes to the polls. He was a non-combatant during the Civil War, the only skirmishes in which he was engaged being with the 'rebellious' and refractory boys of his school at Linneus, infrequent in number and not serious in character. His father served under General Price a portion of the time during the war.

"The fine telescope now in the University observatory was adjusted by Professor Ficklin, who is its chief master and most frequent visitor. He is a thoroughly practical astronomer; is at home in every department of mathematical science, whether it relates to the solution of arithmetical problems or a discussion on the processions of the equinoxes."

Joseph Ficklin died 6 September, 1887, and Penelope, his wife, died 19 October, 1893. Both are buried in the cemetery at Columbia, Missouri. Their children are:

> 487. Octavia, who was born in Trenton, Missouri, 15 September, 1862. She graduated from the University of Missouri in 1882. 14 October, 1885, she married Willard Percy Cave, a prominent attorney of Moberly, Missouri, of which city he was thrice mayor. Octavia Cave died in Moberly, 11 October, 1892, and is buried in Columbia, Missouri. To this union were born three daughters: (a) Catherine Ficklin Cave, who in 1907 married Malcolm McClellan, resides in Jacksonville, Florida, and has two children; (b) Helen Mar Cave, who married Homer Cresap Teachenor, 11 October, 1911. They live at Shelbina, Missouri; (c) Penelope Cave, who died in infancy and is buried at Moberly.
>
> [Mr. Cave afterwards married Miss Fannie P. Lango. They have a son, Harold Sergius Cave. All reside in Moberly.]
>
> 488. Eleanor, who was born in Columbia, 16 June, 1865. She graduated from the University of Missouri in 1885. 3 September, 1890, she married Dr. John

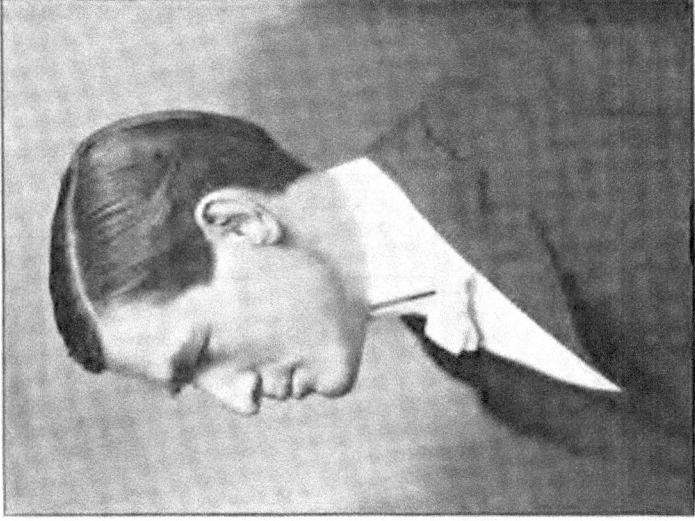

Walter Homan Ficklin of Littleton, Colorado, and Wife, Mabel Rowlett (Kenmuir) Ficklin.

Waldo Connaway, who has for many years been a professor in the University of Missouri, and whose valuable investigations of infectious diseases of live-stock has attracted world-wide attention. They have one daughter, Penelope Connaway, who was born 19 August, 1891.

489. John Bowman, who was born in Columbia, 26 March, 1868. He married Miss Isabelle McClement of Bates county, Missouri, 24 July, 1895, and resides in Denver, Colorado, where he is connected with one of the leading real estate firms of that city. They have one daughter: Isabelle Annette, born 11 April, 1906.

490. Thomas Allen, who was born in Columbia, 8 December, 1870. 29 September, 1897, he married Miss Ella Cochel, daughter of William and Charlotte Cochel of Columbia. They have no children. Mr. Ficklin is engaged in the land title business and has interests in Florida.

491. Walter Homan, the compiler of this book, was born in Columbia, Missouri, 9 April, 1873. He graduated from the University of Missouri, Class of 1895, and in 1896 moved to Kansas City, where he was instructor in biology in Central High School of that place. 29 June, 1898, he married Miss Mabel Rowlett Kenmuir, who was born 7 July, 1877.†

In 1901 they moved to Littleton, Colorado, where Mr. Ficklin was superintendent of schools, and was later, for several years, connected with the Wolcott School in Denver. They still reside in Littleton, and have one child: Joseph Kenmuir, a promising lad of eight years, born 5 October, 1903.

†Mabel Rowlett Kenmuir is a daughter of the late James Piper Kenmuir and wife, Celia Helen (Rowlett), who were married in Kansas City, 6 February, 1876.

Mr. Kenmuir, a pioneer merchant of Kansas City, was born 6 April, 1837, at Ballinahinch, County Galway, Ireland, and died in Kansas City, 9 September, 1902, and is buried in Forest Hill cemetery of that place.

Mrs. Celia (Rowlett) Kenmuir is a daughter of the late Reverend James A. Rowlett, of North Urbana, New York, and wife, Maria Ann, daughter of John Bradford Mitchell. Mrs. Kenmuir resides in Kansas City, where she and her daughter, Nellie, are very prominent in church and club circles.

492. Mary, who was born in Columbia, 22 August, 1875. She attended the public schools of Columbia, and later entered Christian College of that place. 29 December, 1897, she was married to Oscar Lee Clark, a merchant of Linneus, Missouri. They afterwards resided in St. Joseph, but Mrs. Clark's failing health compelled them to move to a milder climate. They went to Denver, but her health steadily declined. She died childless 8 July, 1905, and is buried in Fairmount cemetery in that city. Mr. Clark has since become a prominent merchant of Liberty, Missouri, where he is a member of the firm of Snelling & Clark. He recently married Mrs. Sophia Hemstreet, of that city.

273. Mary Ellen Ficklin, daughter of Joseph, Sr., and Eleanor Wilson (Brown) Ficklin, married David Benson. Their home was at Trenton, Missouri. She died in 1855, whilst on a visit in Kansas, and is buried in Trenton. They had two children:

493. Mark Benson, who is living in Union county, Oregon.
494. Ellen Benson, who married D. B. Beard and has two children. They reside in Keating, Baker county, Oregon.

Mr. Benson married a second wife and is living in Baker City, Oregon.

274. Sarah Ann Ficklin, daughter of Joseph, Sr., and Eleanor Wilson (Brown) Ficklin, married Rue White, a nephew of her stepmother. Mr. White enlisted in the Confederate Army in 1861, and is thought to have been killed in the Battle of Pea Ridge, but his fate has never been definitely ascertained. They had no children. Mrs. White resides in Columbia, Missouri, with her sister, Mrs. Newman.

275. James William Ficklin, son of Joseph, Sr., and Eleanor Wilson (Brown) Ficklin, was born in Mercer county, Kentucky, in 1842, and died in 1880, in Colusa, California, where he is buried. In 1861, he enlisted in Confederate Army from Trenton, Missouri, and served

throughout the Civil War, being in many of the principal engagements, such as Shiloh, Chattanooga, etc. In 1865, when "Jimmy" returned from the war, he was elected marshal of Columbia, and held that trying position for several years and experienced many exciting encounters during those troublous times. He never married.

276. Nancy Ficklin, daughter of Joseph, Sr., and Eleanor Wilson (Brown) Ficklin, died when five years of age.

277. John Cecil Ficklin, son of Joseph, Sr., and Eleanor Wilson (Brown) Ficklin, died in 1851, whilst the family was emigrating from Kentucky to Missouri.

278. Catherine Ficklin, daughter of Joseph, Sr., and Eleanor Wilson (Brown) Ficklin, was born in Mercer county, Kentucky, 18 January, 1849, and emigrated with her father to Grundy county, Missouri, in 1851. She married Cassius Calhoun Newman, of Boone county, and they have ever since resided in Columbia. Mr. Newman has for many years been a most successful merchant and one of the foremost citizens of Central Missouri, taking at all times an active interest in public affairs. Their children are:

495. Edna Earl Newman, who married Samuel S. Johnston and resides at Coweta, Oklahoma. They have an infant son, Lawrence Newman Johnston.

496. Roy Ficklin Newman, who is a prosperous hardware merchant in Moberly, Missouri.

497. Nellie Newman, who married Charles E. Trumbo of Linneus, Missouri. They reside in Wagoner, Oklahoma, and have no children.

498. Ethel Newman, married Claude H. Thomas, who is associated in business with Mr. Newman in Columbia. They have two young children: Marjorie Thomas and Claude Thomas, Jr.

499. Arthur Holland Newman is connected with the Koken Supply Company of St. Louis. He married Miss Minnie Koken of St. Louis, and has one infant son, Ernest Koken Newman.

279. Taylor Ficklin, twin of Catherine (No. 278) died in infancy, and is buried beside his mother.

280. Nellie Ficklin, daughter of Joseph, Sr., and his second wife, Nancy (Carter) Ficklin, married John H. Cook, lately deceased, and resides at Colusa, California. She had six children:

        500.   Luella Cook, who is dead.

        501.   John D. Vincil Cook.

        502.   Florence Cook.

        503.   Nellie Cook.

        504.   Magna Cook.

        505.   Evangeline Cook.

281. Annie Ficklin, daughter of Joseph, Sr., and his second wife, Nancy (Carter) Ficklin, married James G. Ford and resides in Tonopah, Nevada. Their children are:

        506.   Hallie Ford, married a Mr. Wheeler and lives in San Francisco.

        507.   Claude Ford, who married Miss Biddle, of Chicago.

        508.   Irene Ford, who married W. H. O'Neill and lives in Tonopah, Nevada.

        509.   Florence Ford, who married J. D. Forman.

        510.   James Ford.

        511.   Annie Ford.

        512.   Leland Ford.

282. Herbert Ficklin, son of Joseph, Sr., and his second wife, Nancy (Carter) Ficklin, died in Maxwell, California, 12 December, 1885, aged 29. He is buried in the cemetery at Colusa, California. He never married.

---

283. William J. Ficklin, son of Robert and Sarah (Shortridge) Ficklin, was born in 1844. He married Miss Barbara Holbrook and resides at Owensboro, Kentucky. They have three children:

        513.   Adeana.

        514.   Clarence.

        515.   Gertrude.

284. Mary Ficklin, daughter of Robert and Sarah (Shortridge) Ficklin, married Samuel Hudson and lives at Livia, Kentucky. They have four children:

    516. Maggie Hudson.
    517. Robert Hudson.
    518. Claud Hudson.
    519. Ray Hudson.

285. Robert Ficklin, Jr., son of Robert and Sarah (Shortridge) Ficklin, married Miss Phoebe Jones and is living at Montrose, Colorado. They have eight children:

    520. Alvens.
    521. Robert.
    522. John.
    523. Birdie.
    524. Virtie.
    525. Edgar.
    526. Catharine.
    527. Goebel.

286. Narcissa Ficklin, daughter of Robert and Sarah (Shortridge) Ficklin, married Richard Humphrey in June, 1884. They are living at Utica, Kentucky, and have no children.

287. Florence Ficklin, daughter of Robert and Sarah (Shortridge) Ficklin, died at age of 17.

288. Susan Ficklin, daughter of Robert and Sarah (Shortridge) Ficklin, married James Murray and lives at Beaver Dam, Kentucky. They have four children:

    528. J. R. Murray.
    529. Charles Murray.
    530. Carl Murray.
    531. Mabel Murray.

289. Sarah Ficklin, daughter of Robert and Sarah (Shortridge) Ficklin, was a twin of Susan, born 8 February, 1857. She married her first cousin, Joseph Ficklin. For further account of this family, see No. 294.

290. Robert Ficklin, son of William T. and Fetna Ann (Fleece) Ficklin, was killed at Little Rock, Arkansas, 9 September, 1863. He was a member of "Merrill's Horse," a regiment of Federal cavalry, organized in North Missouri.

291. Nicholas F. Ficklin, son of William T. and Fetna Ann (Fleece) Ficklin, was born in Danville, Kentucky, 28 January, 1843. He emigrated with his parents to Trenton, Missouri, in 1852. In 1861 he joined the Missouri State Guards (Confederate), then on their way from Springfield to Lexington. He enlisted in Captain Small's Company, and was present at the siege of Lexington. Here a battery was formed from cannon captured and Captain Churchill Clark was placed in command. Nicholas F. joined this battery. He was at the Battle of Pea Ridge, where Captain Clark was slain and also in the Battles of Corinth and Iuka, and was with Johnston in front of Vicksburg. He was taken prisoner at Bolivar Landing, Mississippi, 25 September, 1863, and taken to Camp Morton, near Indianapolis, where he was imprisoned until May, 1865, and then released.

In that year he crossed the plains to Salt Lake with an ox team, conveying supplies for the United States government. Three and a half months were consumed in the trip from St. Joseph to Salt Lake. He received fifty-three cents per pound for freight. He then made his way to Union, Oregon, where he continued for a while in the freighting business, but later engaged in farming and stock raising. He has recently retired from active business and moved to Portland with his family. He married Miss Susan Christian. Their children are:

532. Mary.
533. Hallie.
534. William T.
535. Margaret.
536. Rose.
537. Bentford.

292. John C. Ficklin, son of William T. and Fetna Ann (Fleece) Ficklin, went to Texas many years ago and is thought to be dead, as he has not been heard from in over thirty years.

293. Mary W. Ficklin, daughter of William T. and Fetna Ann (Fleece) Ficklin, married Joel P. Kinnison, and lives at Baker City, Oregon.

294. Joseph Ficklin, son of William T. and Fetna Ann (Fleece) Ficklin, was born 28 October, 1851. He married his first cousin, Sarah A. Ficklin (No. 289), and resides at Diamond, Washington. They have two children:
>   538. Georgia, born 28 August, 1893.
>   539. Henry, born 7 February, 1896.

295. George D. Ficklin, twin of Joseph (No. 294), is dead.

296. Jared, (297) Sandusky D., and (298) Thomas, sons of William T. and Fetna Ann (Fleece) Ficklin. Nothing has been learned concerning them.

299. John Caldwell Fleece, son of Dr. Clinton B. and Sarah (Ficklin) Fleece, died in Arkansas City, Kansas, in April, 1906.

300. Elizabeth H. Fleece, daughter of Dr. Clinton B. and Sarah (Ficklin) Fleece, married Hardin B. Perkins, and raised a family. Mr. Perkins died about 1900. His widow and family live near Baker City, Oregon. There were five children.

301. William Hamilton Fleece, son of Dr. Clinton B., and Sarah (Ficklin) Fleece, was born 10 February, 1845. He is living in Portland, Oregon. He married Elizabeth Kennedy. They had four children:
>   540. Mary Hundley, who married Geo. W. Robbins of the U. S. Indian service and lives at Warm Springs, Oregon. They have three children: Urban Grant, Ada Elizabeth and George Percival.
>   541. Joseph, who died when a child.
>   542. Lulu Agnes, died in infancy.
>   543. Minnie Pearl, married W. T. Masters and lives in Baker City, Oregon. They have no children.

311. James Graham Ficklin, son of Col. John and Sarah (Graham) Ficklin, was born in Kentucky, 20 January, 1849, and died at King City, Missouri, 25 March, 1906. He married Mary Pillow Dawson, April,

1873. They had no children, but reared two orphans: Waller Bean, who married Mollie Liggett and lives at Winchester, Kentucky, and Julia Howard, who goes by the name of Julia Howard Ficklin, and is at present attending the Orphan School at Midway, Kentucky.

James G. Ficklin served as sheriff of Bath county, Kentucky, for a term of years.

312. Thomas Ficklin, son of Col. John and Sarah (Graham) Ficklin, was born in Kentucky, 29 January, 1851. 28 January, 1873, he was married in Bath county to Mary Young, daughter of L. W. and Emily Young. Thomas Ficklin is a progressive and prosperous farmer of Stanberry, Missouri. He has six children:

544. Arthur Graham, who is a graduate of the University of Missouri, class of 1900. In October, 1907, he married Frances Alexander, daughter of Judge Joshua Alexander of Gallatin, Missouri, who is a member of Congress from that state. He has no children, and is a farmer and stockman living at Jamesport, Missouri.

545. Charles Lee, who married Nona Crenshaw of Maysville, Missouri, and is editor and publisher of the "DeKalb County Herald," published in Maysville, where he resides. They have a little daughter, Martha Margaret.

546. James G., Jr., who married Leonore Ross, daughter of William Ross, of Stanberry, Missouri. They live near King City and have two children: Helen Belle, seven years of age, and William Graham, three years old.

547. Nancy Young, who married in 1907, Joseph Newton Darnell of Tennessee. Mr. Darnell is a Christian minister, with a pastorate at Trenton, Kentucky. They have one child, an infant son.

548. Henry Stone, who is 28 years of age, a minister and not married.

549. Sarah Ann, who is attending Ward Seminary at Nashville, Tennessee.

313. Margaret M. Ficklin, daughter of Col. John and Sarah (Graham) Ficklin, married S. G. Hazelrigg, who died in 1895. They had two daughters:

    550. Ella Graham Hazelrigg, who is teaching school at Union Starr, Missouri.

    551. Kittie Hughes Hazelrigg, who recently married Fred G. Thomas, and lives with her mother at Maryville, Missouri.

314. Ellen Ficklin, daughter of Col. John and Sarah (Graham) Ficklin, married John L. McCormick of Mt. Sterling, Kentucky. They have also a winter home in Florida. To them were born five children:

    552. Minnie Graham McCormick, who married B. F. Chenault of Mt. Sterling, Kentucky. They have two children: Elise Belle, aged 9, and Wesley, aged 5.

    553. Leslie McCormick, who married Lilly Barnes and lives at Mt. Sterling. They have two children: Graham, aged 8, and Pearl, aged 5.

    554. Ollie McCormick, who married Sallie Gaitskill and lives in Mt. Sterling. They have one child, John Gaitskill, aged 5.

    555. Frank Allen McCormick, who married Anna Taul, and lives in Mt. Sterling. They have no children.

    556. Stuart McCormick, who is 18 years of age, and living with his parents.

315. John Ficklin, son of Col. John and Sarah (Graham) Ficklin, lives in Illinois. He married Miss Hopkins, who died in 1895, leaving two children:

    557. Annie May, who was recently married.

    558. Flora Zaye, who lives at Iowa City, Iowa, with her grandparents.

316. Sarah Ficklin, daughter of Col. John and Sarah (Graham) Ficklin, married S. M. Young, brother of Mary Young (No. 312). They live on a farm in DeKalb county, Missouri, and have five children:

    559. Dawson Young.

> 560. John Young.
> 561. Sarah Ann Young.
> 562. Lewis Young.
> 563. Clara Margaret Young.

317. Robert Lee Ficklin, son of Col. John and Sarah (Graham) Ficklin married Emma Carver of Clinton county, Missouri. They live at S Joseph, Missouri, and have one child:
> 564. Emma Lee, aged four years.

318. Stuart Ficklin, son of Col. John and Sarah (Graham) Ficklin, marrie Anna Follett of Gentry county, Missouri, and lives near King City Missouri, on a farm. They had five children:
> 565. Hazel, died when 12 years of age.
> 566. Harry.
> 567. Zoe.
> 568. Jennie.
> 569. Florence.

319. Henry Walker Ficklin, son of Col. John and Sarah (Graham) Ficklin married Harrietta Staley of Gentry county, Missouri, and lives at Stan berry, Missouri. They have three young children:
> 570. Maggie May.
> 571. William Virgil.
> 572. James Thomas.

320. Kate Ficklin, daughter of Col. John and Sarah (Graham) Ficklin married Albert Sidney Hillix, and lives at Weston, Missouri. The have two children:
> 573. Albert Hillix, Jr.
> 574. Gladys Hillix.

---

332. William W. Ficklin, son of Christopher DeAtley and Louisa (Frank lin) Ficklin, is now dead. He served in the 9th Virginia Cavalry, C S. A., 1861-1865. He married Miss Rockwell. They had five chil dren:
> 575. William, Jr.

576. Thomas Dorsey.
577. Millard F., lives at Farnham, Virginia.
578. Dora, married W. A. Bryant, and lives near Warsaw, Richmond county, Virginia.
579. Lloyd, who lives in Missouri.

333. Thomas Dorsey Ficklin, son of Christopher DeAtley and Louisa (Franklin) Ficklin, was first lieutenant in the 40th Virginia Infantry, C. S. A., 1861-1865. He married Miss Lyell, and resided in Lancaster county, Virginia. Their children are as follows:
580. Richard Lyell, who lives at Ottoman, Virginia.
581. Thomas Dorsey, who lives at Litwalton, Virginia.
582. Louisa.
583. Annie, who married T. Beale Marston, and resides in Tappahannock, Essex county, Virginia.
584. Jennie. } Twins.
585. John.

334. Virginia Ficklin, daughter of Christopher DeAtley and Louisa (Franklin) Ficklin, married William C. Oldham, who was for many years sheriff of Richmond county, Virginia. Three of their children are living:
586. Louisa Oldham.
587. Sallie Oldham.
588. Thomas Oldham.

335. Eugene D. Ficklin, son of Christopher DeAtley, and his second wife, Mary (Wright) Ficklin, served in the 40th Virginia Infantry, C. S. A., and was wounded in the Battle of Bull Run. He married a Mrs. Dorsey of Fairfax county, Virginia, and resides in Vinita, Craig county, Oklahoma, where he is a county official. He has several daughters and a son:
589. Samuel.

336. Theodore H. Ficklin, son of Christopher DeAtley and his second wife, Mary (Wright) Ficklin, was born 13 March, 1846, was lieutenant-colonel of the 40th Virginia Infantry, C. S. A., and surrendered with General Lee at Appomattox. He took the degree of Master of Arts at Georgetown University in 1869. He married Miss Susannah Libby

Carne of Alexandria. He has been principal of the George Washington High School in Alexandria, Virginia, since 1871. To this union were born thirteen children, eight of whom died in infancy. Those living reside in Alexandria and are as follows:

590. Jean V., who is employed in the adjutant general's office of the United States war department. He married Miss Javins and has four children: Benjamin Slaughter, Madelaine, Elizabeth and Rosemary.

591. Mary Joseph Kroes.

592. Cecelia.

593. Mary Fitzhugh.

594. Mildred Thornton, who married Thomas J. Echols of Atlanta, Georgia, who is employed in Washington, and resides in Alexandria. They have an infant daughter, Mary Echols, born 5 August, 1909.

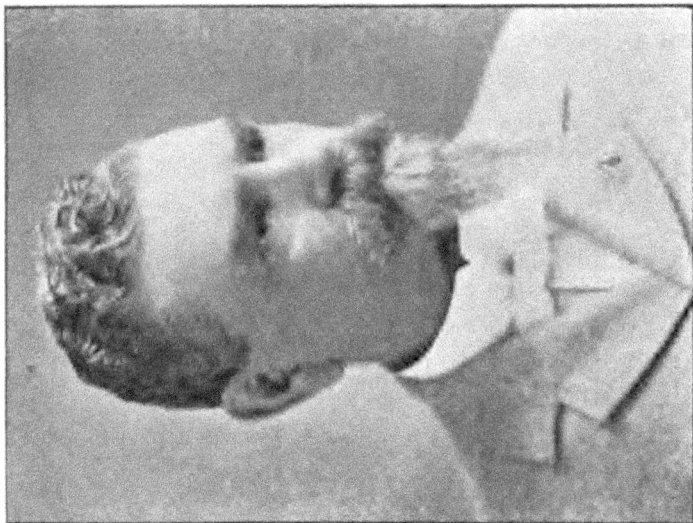

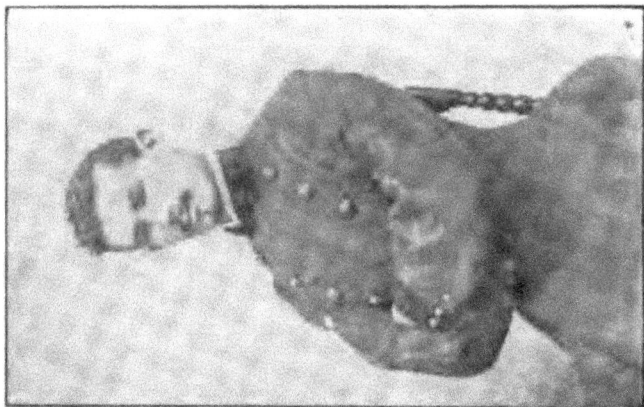

1   2

1. Colonel Theodore H. Ficklin, of Alexandria, Virginia.
2. Colonel Ficklin in Uniform of Confederate Infantry Officer, Army of Northern Virginia, 1863-1865.

CHAPTER IX.

A MANUSCRIPT ACCOUNT OF THE FICKLIN FAMILY BY WILLIAM
SLAUGHTER, OF FREDERICKSBURG, VIRGINIA, 1860.

(The original manuscript is in the possession of H. C. Ficklen, of Danville, Virginia, grandson of
William Slaughter.)

The first of the Ficklen's in Virginia was Benjamin, who came from
England a young man and settled in King George.

A brother, named George, stopped at Bermuda.   It is thought he went
to South Carolina, and was the ancestor of all of that name in that quarter.

Benjamin was ancestor of all those in Virginia, and who moved from
Virginia.

Benjamin had four sons who married and settled in Virginia: William,
Thomas, Anthony and Benjamin.

William lived near Fredericksburg in Spottsylvania; Thomas lived and
died in King George.

Anthony and Benjamin lived near each other in Poplar Settlement, Stafford, 10 miles from Falmouth.

William had a son who died in Quebec.   Thomas and John and Joe,
his sons, all went to Kentucky.

Thomas had an only son, John, who moved to Maysville, and died there.
He left two or three sons there.

Anthony had three sons: Charles, Benjamin and Lewis, all died in Virginia.   Philips son of Lewis.

Benjamin had four sons: Fielding, Daniel, William and Benjamin.

Thomas, son of William, had three sons: Joseph, William and John, the
last a Baptist preacher.

John, nothing known of his sons.

Joe had a son named Robert. I once saw him in Culpeper.

Daniel's sons were Noble, William, James, Daniel. Noble is dead; left a son and daughter.

No knowledge of William Ficklin's daughter.

Thomas, the elder, had two daughters, who married Sweatmans *(sic)*, another married Duff, went to Kentucky. Another married a Matthews, and died in Virginia.

Anthony had four daughters: Frances married Duncan, left no issue. Elizabeth married Stewart, both dead, left a son and daughter who went to Missouri. Mildred never married. Susan married Bell. He is dead. She and family went to Missouri.

Benjamin had four daughters: Mary married a White, left only one daughter, who married N. Fant Another daughter married F. Bell, moved to Wheeling, leaving four sons and one daughter. Susan married Edward Matthews—no children. Elizabeth married Dr. Elbert, went to Ohio, died leaving one son and two daughters.

Benjamin had four sons: Fielding, Daniel, William and Benjamin.

[The remainder of the manuscript deals exclusively with the later generations of the branch of which Benjamin Ficklen, youngest son of the immigrant, was ancestor, and appears in a more complete form in Slaughter W. Ficklin's pamphlet, printed at Charlottesville, Virginia, in 1870.—W. H. F.]

CHAPTER X.

A SYNOPSIS OF OLD RECORDS.

King George County, Virginia.

1736. Deed of lease from Scarlet Hancock to John Tayloe mentions William Ficklin.

1736. (26 March.) Deed of re-lease from Scarlet Hancock to John Tayloe describes land on which William Ficklin lived.

1745. (27 May.) Deed of lease from John Tayloe to William Ficklin and wife, Sarah.

1754. (16 April.) Will of Charles Bruce mentions sons, Wm. Bruce, Charles Bruce; and daughters, Susannah Fickling, Elizabeth Bruce, Mary Bruce, Frances Bruce, and Margaret Bruce.

1756. (2 November.) Deed of gift from Sarah Fickling *et als.* to Benjamin Fickling.

1759. Deed of lease from Zachariah Underwood to Thomas Ficklin.

1778. (9 June.) Deed of gift from Thomas Ficklin to son-in-law, William Jenkins.

1778. (21 November.) Will of Thomas Ficklin mentions daughters, Susannah Sweetnaim, Ann Fewell, Margaret Jenkins, Sarah Swetnam, Elizabeth Ficklin, and Lucy Ficklin; son, John Ficklin; sons-in-law, Wm. Sweetnaim and John Swetnam; brother, Benjamin Ficklin; nephew, James Bowen; grandson, Lewis Bell.

1785. Deed from John Ficklin and John Gravatt to Francis Fitzhugh.
The older marriage records of this county were stolen or destroyed during the Civil War.

Spottsylvania County, Virginia.

1759. (4 February.) Will of Edward Herndon, wit. William Ficklin, James Williams, John Herndon.

1765. (22 July.) Will of Margeret Bruce, spinster, mentions her four sisters, Mary James, Susannah Fickling, Elizabeth Bronaugh, and Frances Banks.

1770. (4 June.) Deed from Wm. Fitzhugh and wife, Ann, to William Ficklin of Spottsylvania county, deeds land in St. George's Parish.

1772. (15 September.) Alexander Spottswood of Spottsylvania county, deeds 220 acres in St. George's Parish to Thomas Ficklin, wife, Mary, and son, John Herndon, of said county.

1781. (30 August.) Wm. Ficklin, of Spottsylvania county, deeds 124 acres in St. George's Parish to Jas. Julian of same county.

1785. (6 September.) At a court held for Spottsylvania county, Thomas Ficklin is declared to be the heir of Charles Ficklin, a soldier of the Continental Army, who died in the service.

1787. (3 July.) Shadrach Moore and Ann, his wife, of Spottsylvania county, deed 169 acres in St. George's Parish to Wm. Smith of Fredericksburg, Joseph Ficklin and others witnesses.

1788. (10 September.) Will of Jarvis Haydon of Spottsylvania county, Ester Ficklin and others witnesses.

1789. (20 April.) Wm. Ficklin, of Spottsylvania county, deeds 200 acres on Rappahannock river in Spottsylvania county to George White of Stafford county.

1790. (23 September.) Will of Roderick White; Fielding Ficklin, Daniel Ficklin and Mary White, executors.

No Ficklin is mentioned in the marriage records of this county prior to 1800.

___

Stafford County, Virginia.

1784. (29 October.) Deed from Anthony Ficklen of Stafford county to son, Charles Ficklen of Fauquier county.

1805. (12 December.) Inventory and appraisement of estate of Benjamin Ficklen; Gabriel Jones, John Sterne and Lewis Ficklen, appraisers.

1805. (13 December.) Account of sales of the estate of Benjamin Ficklen, deceased, of Stafford county; Fielding Ficklen, administrator.

1809. (24 May.) Deed from Benjamin Ficklen and Robert Crutcher to Elijah Hansbrough and Geo. Lane.

1813. (19 January.) Benjamin George and Wm. Robinson convey land to Benjamin Ficklen.

1813. (10 April.) Benjamin Ficklen and wife, Susannah, of Stafford county, convey land to Wm. R. Gordon.

1825. (3 September.) Thornton Patton and others convey to Strother Ficklin.

1825. (21 November.) Strother Ficklen conveys land to Thomas Stewart.

1826. (10 July.) Letter of attorney from Richard Simms to Lewis Ficklen.

1826. (22 July.) Deed from Geo. Tackett to Strother Ficklen.

1826. (5 December.) Account of sales of William Ficklen.

1844. (4 January.) Marriage contract of Leonard H. Ficklen of Stafford county and Terressa F. Hill of Fauquier county.

All marriage records of this county, prior to 1856, were destroyed during the Civil War.

Culpeper County, Virginia.

1798. Deed from Fielding Ficklin to Gordon.

1808. Deed from Fielding Ficklin to J. Eggborn.

1809. Will of Fielding Ficklin.

1813. Deed from George Ficklin to Fenwick.

1816. Deed from Benj. Ficklin to Ficklin.

1818. Deed from Geo. Ficklin to Jno. P. Fant.

1832. Cyrus Ficklin to Chilton.

1835-45. Appraisement and administrator's settlement of estate of Cyrus Ficklin.

1854. Appraisement and administrator's settlement of estate of George Ficklin.

The following marriages are on record in this county:

1787. Benjamin Ficklin to Susannah Foushee.

1813. Harriet Ficklin to Wm. Slaughter.

1816. Benjamin Ficklin to Eleanor Slaughter.

1820. Eliza Ficklin to Mark Read.

1835. Elizabeth Ficklin to Thos. Hill.

1846. Frances M. Ficklin to A. J. Coons.

Fauquier County, Virginia.

1798. (19 October.) John Ficklin of Fauquier county conveys slaves to Fielding Ficklin. Mentions estate of James Kinyon.

1798. (19 September.) Travers Daniel, Sr., James Wint, trustee of estate of James Kenyon, John Ficklin and Judith, his wife, convey to Wm. Beale.

1798. Wm. Ficklin conveys to Wm. W. Peyton, trustee.

1800. Thos. James conveys to Charles Ficklin.

1801. Joseph Anderson *et als.* convey to Charles Ficklin.

1816. Will of Charles Ficklin mentions wife, Mary; children, Anthony Strother Ficklin, Charles B. Ficklin, Betsy Ficklin, Susan B. Ficklin, Polly Foushe, Maria P. Ficklin, Nancy Fant, and Drucilla Harriet Ficklin; sons-in-law, Philip Foushe, George Buckner Fant.

1816. Charles B. Ficklin, appraisement.

1817. Chas. Ficklin, appraisement.

1819. Chas. B. Ficklin, administrator's account.

1828. Will of Lewis Ficklin.

1829. Deed from Wm. Hill to Mildred Ficklin.

1833. Chas. Ficklin, exors. account.

1833. Chas. and Mary Ficklin, sale list.

1834. Chas. and Mary Ficklin, appraisement.

1834. Chas. Ficklin, administrator, conveys to Thos. H. Boswell.

1835. Wm. P. Ficklin, trustee, conveys to Wm. S. Deneale.

1836. Wm. P. Ficklin conveys to R. C. L. Moncure, trustee.

1838. Lewis Ficklin, appraisement.

1843. Lewis Ficklin, division of slaves.

1843. Will of Frances M. Ficklin.

1844. A. S. Ficklin, appraisement.

1844. Anthony S. Ficklin, sale list.

1844. Frances M. Ficklin, appraisement.

1846. Anthony S. Ficklin, administrator's account.

1846. Wm. P. Ficklin, Trustee, conveys to George Latham.

1848. Anthony S. Ficklin, administrator's account.

1850. Anthony S. Ficklin, administrator's account.
The older records of this county show but one Ficklin marriage—
that of S. Ficklin to G. B. Fant, 15 December, 1815.

Richmond County Virginia.

1793. (27 September.) Will of Christopher DeAtley mentions wife,
Eleanor DeAtley, and daughters, Elizabeth Ficklin, wife of
Famous Ficklin, and Sarah Hogan, wife of Travers Hogan.
1824. (31 January.) Will of Ann Ficklin mentions brothers, Christopher
D. Ficklin and Leroy D. Ficklin, and sister, Sallie Ficklin.
1830. (4 October.) Will of Sarah Ficklin mentions brothers, Christopher
D. Ficklin and Leroy D. Ficklin.
1834. (6 January.) Will of Leroy D. Ficklin mentions Sarah Ficklin.
1841. (3 June.) Will of John D. Ficklin mentions brother, Christopher
D. Ficklin.
1836-1848. There are several deeds from Christopher DeAtley Ficklin to
sundry grantees.
1850. (2 December.) Bond of Wm. C. Oldham, guardian for Eugene
D. and Hamilton Theodore Ficklin.

Prince William County, Virginia.

Name Ficklin does not appear on records. Marriage records, prior to
1865, destroyed during Civil War.

Virginia Land Office.

Warrant No. 3879, for 100 acres of land, was issued 20 May, 1785,
to Thomas Ficklin, heir at law of Charles Ficklin, a private of the
Continental Line, who died in the service.

House of Burgesses.

Journal of 1752-1758, page 121 (edited by H. R. McIlwaine).
1753. (14 November.) Resolution was passed in Virginia House of Bur-
gesses rewarding Thomas Ficklin and others for taking up run-
aways.

Jessamine County, Kentucky.

1813. (19 October.) Deed from Robt. Johnson to John Ficklin.
1818. (16 July.) Deed from John Ficklin and wife to Mason Singleton.
1819. (19 April). Will of John Ficklin mentions wife, Mary, and children, Jarrot Ficklin, Betsy Hampton, John Ficklin, William Ficklin, Thomas Ficklin, Sucky Ficklin, Charles Ficklin, Joel Ficklin, Kitty Ficklin, Price Ficklin and Polly Ficklin, also daughter, Sally Payton, her husband, Benjamin Payton, and child, Patsy. Executors—wife, Polly Ficklin, and son, Jarrot Ficklin.
1828. (25 September.) Deed from Henry Morehead to Joseph Ficklin. The name Ficklin does not appear on the older marriage records of this county.

Scott County, Kentucky.

Most of the older records of this county have been destroyed by fire. Those which remain are fragmentary or illegible. There are a few deeds of comparatively recent dates in which the Ficklins are principal parties. No Ficklin wills. There is an account of settlement of estate of Thomas Ficklin, but date cannot be made out. Name does not appear on the marriage records prior to 1837.

Allen County, Kentucky.

Older records destroyed by fire.

Fayette County, Kentucky.

There are no Ficklin wills or settlements of estates, excepting the will of Polly L. Ficklin, probated in 1849, in which she emancipates all her slaves and appears to have devised all her property to them. She speaks of her husband as being then living, but does not mention his first name.

There are also sundry deeds which mention Claressa Ficklin, John H. Ficklin, Joseph Ficklin, Orlando B. Ficklin, Polly Ficklin, Thomas Ficklin and William Ficklin, and a marriage contract between Joseph Ficklin and Polly L. Campbell.

Mason County, Kentucky.

1803.   (30 September.)   Will of John Ficklin mentions wife, Judith, sons, Henry Kenyon Ficklin, Joseph Kenyon Ficklin, John Minton Ficklin, Thomas Ficklin, James Kenyon Ficklin, and Robert Ficklin; daughters, Lucy Ficklin, and Judith Kenyon Ficklin.   Will mentions, also, Fielding Ficklin of Virginia.

Boyle and Mercer Counties, Kentucky.

The name appears in documents of comparatively recent dates, only, in Boyle county and in Mercer, of which Boyle was once a part.

Fleming County, Kentucky.

There are probably some interesting documents on record in this county concerning Daniel Ficklen, but no search of these records proved to be necessary in the preparation of this volume.

Colleton and Beaufort Counties, South Carolina.

All the older records of these counties were destroyed by General Sherman's troops in 1865.

South Carolina Land Office.

1752.   (13 March.)   To Jeremiah Fickling a grant of thirty-eight acres on North Edisto river in Colleton county.

1752.   (22 May.)   To Jeremiah Fickling four hundred fifty acres on Tee Dee river in eastern portion of state.

1767.   To Thomas Fincklen four hundred acres.

1771.   (28 November.)   To Samuel Fickling of Edisto Island twelve hundred fifty acres on the coast.

A Few Federal Census Returns.

Returns for Virginia and Kentucky at the census of 1790, and also of 1800, were destroyed when the National Capitol was burned by the British troops in 1814.   In lieu of the returns for Virginia at the census of 1790, the Bureau of the Census has published what remains of the returns of the Virginia state census, 1782-1785. The returns for many counties, however, are missing.   Anthony and Benjamin Ficklen are shown to have been living in Stafford in 1785.   At the census of 1810 the name does not appear in the returns for Spottsylvania county, but Strother Ficklin, over 16 and under 26; Lewis Ficklin, over 26 and under 45; and Benjamin Ficklin, over 45, are shown to have been heads of families in Stafford at that time.   When the census of 1810 was taken in Kentucky, no one of the name resided in Fayette county.   In Scott county were Thomas Ficklin and wife, both over 45.   In Jessamine county were Jarrott Ficklin, over 26 and under 45, and wife, over 16 and under 26, and one son, under 10, and also John Fickland and wife, both over 45.

When the census of 1790 was taken in South Carolina, the following of the name appeared as heads of families: Beaufort district, Mary Ficklin, William Ficklin; Colleton county, St. John's Parish, Francis Fickling, George Fickling, George Fickling, Jr., 2 James Fickling, Joseph Fickling, Mrs. Fickling (old).

Some Old Records in England.

Norfolk county.
Norfolk Archdeaconry Court.   Wills.
1626.   Alice Fitlinge, Hingham.
1626.   John Fitlinge, Hingham.
1629.   Ralph Fitlinge, Wymondham.
1640.   Ralph Fitlinge, Wymondham.
1664.   John Ficklinge, Witton.
1708.   Benjamin Fitlinge, Bedingham.
1710.   Thomas Fitlinge, Wymondham.

1758.   Thomas Fitlinge, Wymondham.

Norfolk Archdeaconry Court.   Administrations.

1671.   Edward Fitlin, Clerk, East Lexham.

1700-01.   Susanna Fickling, Norwich.

1710.   Robert Fickling, Horsford.

Consistory Court of Norwich.   Wills.

1629.   Robert Ficklin, Sparham.

1637.   Robert Ficklinge, Foulsham.

1662.   John Fytling, Hingham.

1727.   William Fickling, Smallburgh.

1766.   John Ficklin, Gorleston.

Norwich Consistory Court.   Administrations.

1710-11.   William Fickling, Gorleston.

1714-15.   William Fetling, Norwich.

1720-21.   Martha Fickling, Great Witchingham.

1746.   John Fitling, Wymondham.

Norwich Archdeaconry Court.   Wills.

1632.   Marie Fickling, Sparham.

1670.   Andrew Fitling, Bawdeswell.

1672.   Mary Fitling, East Lexham.

1687.   Anne Fickling, Norwich.

1705.   Robert Fickellen, Tuttington.

1707.   John Filkin, Yarmouth.

1713.   William Fickling, St. Faiths.

Miscellaneous Items.

In the Hearth tax of 1674, William Ficklin, cottager, paid on two hearths at Peasenhall, Suffolk, and ——— Ficklinge paid on three hearths at Weybread.

In 1639-40 John Fitling paid 20s toward the ship money tax in Suffolk, Parish of Rockinghall Superior.

In 1705 Willyam Fickling, of Ludham, and Frances Stibburne of Ridlington, were married at East Ruston, Norfolk.

In 1700 Roger Fickling, singleman, of Horsford, and Mary Hase, singlewoman, of Horsford, were married at Marsham, Norfolk.

Buried at Horsford, near Norwich, 9 September, 1746, Robart Ficklen; 15 November, 1767, Elizabeth Ficklen.

At North Elmham are the baptisms and burials of several children of Edward Fitlinge and Katherine, his wife, from 1599 to 1615, including a Robert, born in 1607.

INDEX TO FICKLIN FAMILY.

INDEX TO PERSONS RELATED TO FICKLIN FAMILY BY MARRIAGE, AND OTHERS

www.ingramcontent.com/pod-product-compliance
Lightning Source LLC
Chambersburg PA
CBHW021159010426

R18062100002B/R180621PG41931CBX00002B/1